RICHARD SCHLATTER, GENERAL EDITOR

Humanistic Scholarship in America

⋙ THE PRINCETON STUDIES ⋘

THE COUNCIL OF THE HUMANITIES
WHITNEY J. OATES, CHAIRMAN
PRINCETON UNIVERSITY

ANTHROPOLOGY

Eric R. Wolf

ART AND ARCHAEOLOGY

James S. Ackerman   Rhys Carpenter

CHINESE PAINTING

Wen Fong

CLASSICS

Eric A. Havelock

ENGLISH LITERATURE

David Daiches

FOREIGN LITERATURE

Henri Peyre

HISTORY

John Higham
Leonard Krieger   Felix Gilbert

LINGUISTICS

Eric P. Hamp   Karl D. Uitti
Rulon Wells

Their Authors

MODERN AMERICAN CRITICISM

Walter Sutton

MUSICOLOGY

Frank Ll. Harrison   Mantle Hood
Claude V. Palisca

THE ORIGINS OF AMERICAN
HUMANISTIC SCHOLARS

Robert H. Knapp

PHILOSOPHY

Roderick M. Chisholm   Herbert Feigl
William K. Frankena   John Passmore
Manley Thompson

RELIGION

Paul Ramsey, ed.
Philip H. Ashby   Robert M. Grant
James M. Gustafson   J. H. Nichols
Harry M. Orlinsky   John E. Smith
Claude Welch

RELIGION, A HUMANISTIC FIELD

Clyde A. Holbrook

The aim of these volumes is to present a critical account of American humanistic scholarship in recent decades. They have been commissioned by the Council of the Humanities, Whitney J. Oates, Chairman, of Princeton University and were made possible by a grant from the Ford Foundation.

—Richard Schlatter, General Editor.

ENGLISH
LITERATURE

܀܀

DAVID DAICHES

DEAN, SCHOOL OF ENGLISH
AND AMERICAN STUDIES
UNIVERSITY OF SUSSEX

PRENTICE-HALL, INC.   ENGLEWOOD CLIFFS   NEW JERSEY

FOREWORD

What is the purpose of humanistic scholarship? What, in fact, does the humanist scholar do?

The job of the humanist scholar is to organize our huge inheritance of culture, to make the past available to the present, to make the whole of civilization available to men who necessarily live in one small corner for one little stretch of time, and finally to judge, as a critic, the actions of the present by the experience of the past.

The humanist's task is to clear away the obstacles to our understanding of the past, to make our whole cultural heritage—primitive, pre-Columbian, African, Asian, aboriginal, Near Eastern, classical, medieval, European, American, contemporary, and all the rest—accessible to us. He must sift the whole of man's culture again and again, reassessing, reinterpreting, rediscovering, translating into a modern idiom, making available the materials and the blueprints with which his contemporaries can build their own culture, bringing to the center of the stage that which a past generation has judged irrelevant but which is now again usable, sending into storage that which has become, for the moment, too familiar and too habitual to stir our imagination, preserving it for a posterity to which it will once more seem fresh.

The humanist does all this by the exercise of exact scholarship. He must have the erudition of the historian, the critical abilities of the philosopher, the objectivity of the scientist, and the imagination of all three. The scholar who studies the history of science, for example, must combine a knowledge of languages, history, and philosophy with the knowledge of a scientist. And so on with the scholars who study music, art, religion, literature, and all the rest.

The job is, obviously, impossible for any man; and the humanist scholar, knowing he can never attain his true goal, is always tempted to run after wooden idols whose cults are less exacting and which proffer an easy bliss.

Sometimes the humanist is tempted to bypass the rigorous training of the scholar and to wrap himself in the cloak of the sophist. Then he lapses into a painful wooliness and becomes the "literary" sort of humanist whose only accomplishment is a style which achieves the appearance of sublimity at the cost of an actual inanity. His opposite number is the hardheaded humanist who reacts against empty loftiness by becoming a pedant: he devotes himself to antiquarian detail no less trivial than the banalities of some social science or the mere collecting spirit which is sometimes found in the natural sciences. "Physical science can be at least as trivial as any other form of inquiry: but this is less obvious to the outsider because the triviality is concealed in the decent obscurity of a learned language."

Given the magnitude of his task and the impossibility of total perfection, the humanist scholar must, of course, specialize and his works will often be esoteric. But the belief persists that somehow specialization must be converted to generalization if the humanist scholar is to complete his job. Humanist scholars have not solved the problems of excessive specialization and must share the blame for that catastrophe of communication which besets modern learning.

viii

Humanist scholars have been accused of being overly gen-
teel, contemptuous of popular culture, snobbish and anti-
democratic after the fashion of their aristocratic Renaissance
progenitors, backward looking, hostile to the present, fearful
of the future, ignorantly petulant about science, technology,
and the Industrial Revolution—"natural Luddites." "It is a
sad thought indeed that our civilization has not produced a
New Vision," a modern technologist complains, "which could
guide us into the new 'Golden Age' which has now become
physically possible, but only physically. . . . Who is responsible for this tragi-comedy of Man frustrated by success? . . .
Who has left Mankind without a vision? The predictable
part of the future may be a job for electronic predictors but
the part of it which is not predictable, which is largely a matter of free human choice, is not the business of the machines,
nor of scientists . . . but it ought to be, as it was in the
great epochs of the past, the prerogative of the inspired humanists." (Dennis Gabor, "Inventing the Future," *Encounter,*
May 1960, p. 15.)

Scholars in the humanities may modestly reject the suggestion that they can ever be the inspired prophets of a new
age. But their scholarship is essential to enable us to distinguish the inspired prophets from the fanatical Pied Pipers.

The Ford Humanities Project under the direction of the
Council of the Humanities of Princeton University is looking
at American humanistic scholarship of recent decades, describing it, and attempting to sift the imaginative, the original, and the admirable from the pedantic, the conventional,
and the superficial.

From the outset it was our intention to invite a number
of distinguished scholars from abroad to contribute to our

studies and in the field of English scholarship Professor Daiches was obviously the ideal choice. Born and educated in Britain and now teaching at the University of Sussex, he has been a professor at Chicago and Cornell and he knows the American scene as well as any native.

The study of letters in the United States has had many critics. We have heard the charge that literary scholars in America often view literature as an object of study instead of an art, that criticism has become the elucidation of a method rather than the elucidation of a work. Again, the *Times Literary Supplement* continues to scorn, with just that slight misapprehension of the real situation which one expects of provincials far removed from the center of activity, the pedantry of American literary scholarship. Professor Daiches discusses these and similar criticisms with magisterial justice and wisdom. This is one of those books that "must be read by every student of the subject."

RICHARD SCHLATTER
General Editor

PREFACE

The following pages do not represent a systematic survey of the whole field of modern American literary scholarship. That field is far too rich for any one person to be able to discuss it all, however superficially. Indeed, merely to read the titles of books and articles in bibliographies of English literature is a long and arduous task. Though my assignment was to write a critical essay on modern American literary scholarship of the last thirty years or so, I have on the whole confined myself to scholarship in English literature, the only subject on which I can claim to speak with any authority. I have avoided linguistics, and even lexicography; I have concentrated on what I know most about; and I have tried to treat the subject in such a way that the account I give provides a fair if not a complete picture.

I have not aimed at a strenuous objectivity. Obviously, my emphases and judgments are colored by my own views of what literary study is and ought to be. Nor have I attempted a chronological survey of work done, beginning with that done on the medieval writers and working on through the Renaissance and the Enlightenment to the present day. I discuss work done on twentieth century literature before work done on Milton, and both these before I discuss work done on Shakespeare. In doing this I have followed the logic of my own perceptions. Beginning with an illustration of some shifts in emphasis, I was led to consider the meaning of these shifts with particular reference to work done on recent literature. Milton then suggested himself as a poet on whom old and new kinds of work were being done simultaneously and also as a subject on which some characteristically American kinds of concern and kinds of corporate effort have been concentrated. I then turned to deal with work done on Shakespeare in order to broaden the discussion and to see as great a variety as possible of modern kinds of American scholarship and criticism at work. And so the process developed. I have not written a special section on each period, but have taken my illustrations as they came to hand. Above all, I must emphasize that I have not been able to mention more than a very small proportion of scholars and works; the omission of the name of a scholar or a book does not mean that I consider him or her unimportant. This essay is not a catalog or a bibliography (even *raisonnée*), categories that result as soon as one begins to make any attempt at all to name everybody and everything of significance. American scholarship has enough lists, and my task has not been to add another. I am aware that this may be regarded as an insurance against the results of ignorance and that a bland assertion that one knows everything but has perforce left much out is neither very convincing nor very decent. Of course I do not know everything, and I have no doubt that there are some important scholars whose names and work I should know or know of but of whom I am unhappily unaware. There are some defects in the following pages that can only be explained by Dr. Johnson's famous reply of "pure ignorance." I feel the less reluctant to admit this when I contemplate the impossibly vast quantity of modern American literary scholarship, so obviously beyond the grasp of a single reader.

I have therefore dwelt most fully on what I know best, and I have adopted an informal and personal style as one way of making quite clear that this is a personal estimate based on one man's reading and thinking. I have referred freely to experiences I have had when teaching at American universities when I have felt that these might illustrate a relevant point about American literary scholarship, and I have also made comparisons (again based on personal experience) between American and British methods when I thought these might be illuminating.

Some readers may wonder why I have rather taken for granted the whole background of the New Criticism and not given a full account of its development or its varieties. This has involved considerable self-restraint, for it is a subject in which I am much interested. I do not feel, however, that such an account comes within my terms of reference; Professor Walter Sutton has written a particular study, in this same series, of *Modern American Criticism*. My concern has been less to discuss the origin and varieties of the New Criticism than to consider how the practice and the preaching of it has affected and is affecting literary study in America.

As for the evaluative aspect of my account, I am afraid that I may appear to avoid commitment by continually moving from "on the one hand" to "on the other hand," seesawing between hailing praiseworthy features and condemning unfortunate tendencies. But this is exactly what any examination of the achievement of modern American literary study makes one do: in reading and contemplating it one's opinion is constantly jerked between enthusiastic admiration and near-despair. Why that is so, and why in the end the pendulum comes to rest nearer the former than the latter mark, is I hope made clear in the following pages.

DAVID DAICHES

CONTENTS

I   SHIFTS IN EMPHASIS   I

2   MILTON   32

3   SHAKESPEARE   49

4   A VARIETY OF INTERESTS
      AND APPROACHES   69

5   LITERARY CRITICISM
      AND LITERARY HISTORY   90

6   CRITICS AS TEACHERS   111

7   BIOGRAPHY AND LETTERS   132

8   THE INDUSTRIOUS SCHOLAR   140

9   THE PAPERBACK REVOLUTION   146

10 THE THEORY AND THE PRACTICE . . .   153

    INDEX   167

xv

SHIFTS IN EMPHASIS

Anybody interested in De Quincey, thumbing through old volumes of *PMLA* in the periodical room of a university library, might have his eye caught by an article in the 1907 volume by W. Y. Durand entitled "De Quincey and Carlyle in Their Relation to the Germans," a pedestrian account of De Quincey's translations from the German and his critical essays on German literature with the lame conclusion that "De Quincey fell far below Carlyle as a champion of Teutonism." If he goes on to roam the stacks looking for more substantial contributions by American scholars of this period to the study of De Quincey he will find almost nothing. (If, however, he looks into Volume 1 of G. M. Gould's *Biographic Clinics,* Philadelphia, 1903, he will find a discussion of the origins of De Quincey's ill-health.) But if he moves forward in time to discover what was being written by American scholars about De Quincey between 1930 and 1960 he can find W. H. Bonner's edition of new De Quincey letters (*De Quincey at Work,* 1936), Horace Eaton's standard biography (*Thomas De Quincey: A Biography,* 1936), S. K. Proctor's carefully worked out discussion of De Quincey's critical notions (*Thomas De Quincey's Theory of Literature,* 1943), and a further study of De Quincey as critic by J. E. Jordan (*Thomas De Quincey: Literary Critic,* 1952).

Or suppose our student in the library is especially interested in American scholarship on Pope. Going back to the bound volumes of *PMLA,* he can find an article by L. M. Mc-Lean in Volume VI (1891) entitled "The Riming System of Alexander Pope," an article by J. W. Tupper in the 1900 volume on "Pope's Imitations of Horace," and that will be about all for the period 1890-1930. In the stacks he will find only J. R. Lounsbury's study of Pope's edition of Shakespeare (*The Text of Shakespeare,* 1906), T. M. Parrot's edition of *The Rape of the Lock and Other Poems* (1906), Louis Bredvold's edition of *Selected Poems* (1926), and J. T. Hillhouse's *The Grub-Street Journal* (1928). For the following year there is Austin Warren's *Alexander Pope as Critic and Humanist,* and after that we are well away—George Sherburn's *The Early Career of Alexander Pope* (1934), R. K. Root's *The Poetical Career of Alexander Pope* (1938), Maynard Mack's many articles that appeared in the 1940's and later as well as his edition of the *Essay on Man* (Volume II of the Twickenham Edition, 1950), W. K. Wimsatt's critical essays (e.g., "Rhetoric and Poems: The Example of Pope" in *English Institute Essays,* 1949), Charles Kerby-Miller's edition of *The Memoirs of Martinus Scriblerus* (1950), D. M. Knight's critical study of Pope's *Iliad* (*Pope and the Heroic Tradition,* 1951), Edna Steeves's edition of the *Peri Bathous* (1952), Aubrey Williams' book on *The Dunciad* (*Pope's Dunciad: A Study of Its Meaning,* 1955), Sherburn's great five-volume edition of Pope's correspondence (1956), and a host of critical and scholarly articles on Pope in a variety of American periodicals, including an application to Pope's poetry of a specific critical tool from the New Criticism ("Tension in Pope's Poetry," by Rebecca Parkin, *University of Kansas City Review,* 1953).

Let me take one more example—Thomas Gray. Gray has

long attracted critics and scholars out of proportion to the volume or magnitude of his work, perhaps because he was such a scholarly poet himself. Our student in the library will find, for the earlier period, W. L. Phelps's *Selections from the Poetry and Prose of Thomas Gray* (1894), which includes G. L. Kittredge's essay on "Gray's Knowledge of Old Norse"; he will also find C. E. Norton's study of *The Poet Gray as a Naturalist* (1903), A. S. Cook's *Concordance* to Gray's poems (1908), C. S. Northup's "Addison and Gray as Travellers" (in *J. M. Hart Studies,* 1910), E. D. Snyder's book on Gray's (and others') Celtic interests (*The Celtic Revival in English Literature, 1760-1800,* 1923), A. L. Reed's study, *The Background of Gray's Elegy* (1924), and W. N. C. Carlton's privately printed "bibliographical and descriptive note" on Gray's "Elegy" (1925).

In the periodical room the student will find little beyond Snyder's first presentation of some of his Celtic material ("Thomas Gray's Interest in Celtic," *Modern Philology,* 1914) and, also in *Modern Philology,* an article by Odell Shepard suggesting that Richard West is the subject of the concluding epitaph in the "Elegy" ("A Youth to Fortune and to Fame Unknown," 1923). In the more recent period he will find a wealth of material. He will discover that Shepard's article was to prove the opening gun in a stimulating controversy over the identity of the subject of the epitaph and so of the meaning and structure of the "Elegy" as a whole. H. W. Starr took up where Shepard left off. ("A Youth to Fortune and to Fame Unknown," *JEGP,* 1949); F. H. Ellis, in "Gray's Elegy: The Biographical Problem in Literary Criticism" (*PMLA,* 1951), held that the dead youth was the stonecutter; Morse Peckham ("Gray's 'Epitaph' Re-

3

visited," *MLN,* 1956) argued for a modified form of this position, while J. H. Sutherland ("The Stonecutter in Gray's *Elegy," Modern Philology,* 1957) objected. An article by Joseph Foladare set the biographical background to Gray's "Sonnet on the Death of Richard West," provided an explication of the poem linked to this background, and related the poem to the conclusion of the "Elegy" ("Gray's 'Frail Memorial' to West," *PMLA,* 1960). Meanwhile, articles in *The Explicator* (three in 1950-51) were explicating the "Elegy" in divers ways before going on to deal with "The Progress of Poesy" (two articles in 1951) and the "Ode on a Distant Prospect of Eton College" (one article in 1951).

Numerous other articles on Gray—bibliographical, influence-chasing, biographical, critical, and interpretative—appeared in American learned journals in the 1930's, 1940's, and 1950's. W. Powell Jones's biographical study, *Thomas Gray Scholar,* appeared in 1937. (The definitive biography is, however, by an Englishman, R. W. Ketton-Cremer, *Thomas Gray: A Biography,* 1955.) The critical and explicatory work on Gray done in America was by far the most important during this period. One of the best known and most influential of all examples of the New Criticism in action is Cleanth Brooks's essay on Gray's "Elegy" ("Gray's Storied Urn"), which appeared in his collection of essays, *The Well Wrought Urn,* 1947.

Can we draw any conclusions from this information? The three authors were not chosen quite at random; they include one great author and two minor writers, one of whom (De Quincey) has not been much read in recent years. The most obvious inference would seem to be that the work done on all three authors by American scholars and critics in the last

4

thirty years or so is altogether more substantial and more interesting than that done in the preceding thirty or forty years. Perhaps nobody today reads De Quincey; but if we want to know exactly who De Quincey was, and why and how he is interesting, it is to modern American scholars that we must turn. The impressive amount of modern American work on Pope includes some of the most sensitive analytic criticism as well as some of the most impressive editorial and biographical scholarship to be found today. On Gray, the main modern American achievement has been critical and explicatory, in an especially lively way. On the whole, the books and articles on the three authors that were produced in the earlier period are both duller and less central.

Are things then getting better and better? The answer depends on what part of the picture you look at. The fact is that a steadily increasing proportion of the world's work in English studies is being done by Americans, who now produce far more in this field than the scholars of any other country. There are many more students and teachers of English at American colleges and universities now than there were in 1900. The increase in the quantity of work done does not therefore in itself indicate anything more than an increase in quantity. Is the increase in centrality and liveliness real, or does it derive from the fact that, there being a so much larger field to choose from, it is not difficult to pick a small proportion of central and lively works out of a vast mass of eccentricity and dullness? In some degree, if we confine ourselves to published work that gets into the bibliographies and if we ignore unpublished Ph.D. theses, we can say that the increase is real. The dull Germanic scholarship of the researcher in English studies who is determined to prove that he can be a thorough, objective, "scientific" collector of facts about literature belongs much more to 1900 than to 1960. The British caricature of the American scholar producing laborious, enormously detailed, and absolutely unreadable works of research is, like most caricatures, out of date.

Nevertheless, we must be careful in making any generalizations about what has been going on in American literary scholarship. Much of the work on Gray mentioned above results from the chance fact that one of Gray's poems, the "Elegy," is both a popular classic and a poem peculiarly susceptible to the kind of analytic and interpretative treatment that modern critics are best trained to apply. There has been relatively little recent sustained American *scholarship* on Gray.

As for De Quincey, Eaton's work is of the first importance but stands alone; Proctor's analysis of his thought is lively but more concerned to show Proctor's ingenuity in finding a system to which he can make De Quincey's critical writings conform than to come to grips with that wayward mind. (René Wellek, in an article on De Quincey's thought in the *Philological Quarterly*, 1944, warned against such oversystematization.) And I have not listed articles on De Quincey's legal troubles (*PMLA*, 1939) or his illness of 1812 (*PMLA*, 1945) or other marginal topics suggestive of the subject hunter.

The impressive body of work on Pope derives from a number of factors—the continuous activity into retirement of a great scholar of an older generation, a scholar who combines the humanistic impulse of the non-Germanic tradition in American literary studies with the meticulous attention to accuracy and to detail characteristic of the best modern editorial and textual scholarship; the revival of interest in and admiration for Pope as part of the antiromantic critical revolution of the twentieth century (Cleanth Brooks's critical essay on *The Rape of the Lock,* "The Case of Miss Arabella Fermor," appeared beside his "Gray's Storied Urn" in *The Well Wrought Urn*) and the appeal of Pope's irony for the New Criticism; and the emergence, to work on Pope, of some younger writers who combine thorough scholarship with sophisticated critical training, which again is related to Pope's appeal to the modern mind.

Of the three writers discussed above, then, only work on Pope combined scholarly centrality with critical provocativeness. Indeed, Pope is almost unique in modern American literary studies in inviting this combination of scholarship and criticism. Still, my earlier conclusion that a cursory survey of work done on these three writers reveals that that done in the later period is altogether more interesting as well as likely to be more central can stand, if it is not pressed into an overwhelming generalization.

One reason that modern American work on older English writers—or at least such work as sees the light—is less likely to be dull or eccentric or irrelevant is that the field of American literature and of twentieth century English (and American) literature has become increasingly available to the Ph.D. student and to the academic seeking a reputation without the necessity of getting up a historical background. The proportion of work done on recent literature is rising all the time, and, together with much that is central and much that is critically brilliant, there is an enormous amount that is worthless—either because it is merely a stodgy compilation, or because it represents a misguided attempt by an insufficiently able critic to produce original critical analyses of particular works, or because it takes a fashionable text or author and runs into the ground some particular modish technique or approach. Twentieth century literature is the happy hunting ground of the less intelligent and the more eccentric—the fools and the freaks, if I may be allowed a breezy but useful exaggeration—of those who have been drawn off the hunt of older English literature.

There were two items on De Quincey by Americans listed in the *PMLA* bibliography for 1957, one of them an unpublished dissertation and the other an article in *The English Romantic Poets and Essayists: A Review of Research,* published by the Modern Language Association; there was none at all for 1958 or for 1959, and for 1960 there were one unpublished thesis and one facsimile autograph. On Gray, there were two articles in 1957 (one was the article on the stonecutter already referred to), one in 1958, none in 1959 or 1960. (I am confining myself to books or articles by American scholars first published in America.) There were six items on Pope in 1957 (including one by an American scholar in a British periodical) and eleven in 1960 (including one by a British scholar in an American periodical). It is worth noting that for the same years there were eleven items on D. H. Lawrence listed in the *PMLA* bibliography for 1957, sixteen for 1958, over fifty for 1959 (though the number is swollen by including the separate articles in *A D. H. Lawrence Miscellany,* edited by H. T. Moore), and eighteen for 1960. In 1959 there were more than fifty items on Joyce and in 1960 more than thirty; there were also more than thirty on Eliot in each of these years, though the evidence suggests that the Eliot industry is now on the decline. In 1959 the number of American items on twentieth century English literature exceeded the number on the nineteenth or any other century, and there were more items on Joyce than on Milton. In 1960 the number of items on twentieth century and on nineteenth century English literature were about the same, although this time there were more on Milton than on Joyce. In both 1959 and 1960 there were well over a thousand items on American literature, representing in each case considerably more than half of the total items for all periods of English literature. In 1959 there were fifty-seven items on Faulkner by Americans—more than on any other writer whom I have checked for that year except Shakespeare (who continues in the lead, with over 130 items in 1959 and 1960). In 1960 the numbers were similar, though Faulkner was down to forty-one—still one of the highest. Melville has been running at around thirty items a year for the last few years, Hawthorne a bit behind with something over twenty.

The acceptance of twentieth century English literature and of American literature as a legitimate field for research has clearly changed the pattern of American literary studies in the last generation. It is in these two areas that we are therefore likely to find the main results of what may be called mass attack. But there are also other factors operating in the study of twentieth century English (or rather British) literature by Americans. An important factor is the Irish-American affinity. Two of the very greatest of modern writers are Irish or Anglo-Irish—Joyce and Yeats. Now, partly because of the large Irish immigration to the United States and the consequent presence there of many critics and scholars with Irish connections or interests, there has been a tre-

9

mendous amount of American work done on these writers. Some of it is done with a special kind of proprietary feeling. Mary and Padraic Colum, Robert Kelly, Maurice Murphy, Herbert McLuhan, Herbert Cahoon, Anthony Kerrigan, John Kelleher, Seon Givens—these are only a few of the Irish names one can pick out from any bibliography of American writings on Joyce. It is not only that Irish Americans who knew Joyce in Ireland or who had a similar childhood background to his give us their knowing version of "the truth" about him; there is also a more widespread and more general commitment to Ireland. The situation is not quite so obvious in American Yeats studies, but it is nevertheless recognizable; Yeats's father, it may be remembered, spent the latter part of his life in New York. It is said that when the barman in Barney Kiernan's pub in Dublin hears a visiting American ask for a drink, he leans over the counter and asks: "Now would it be Joyce or Yeats you are after?"

One must not, however, exaggerate the importance of American sympathy for and interest in Ireland as an element in helping to account for the mass of American work done on Joyce and Yeats. After all, more work has also been done on Dylan Thomas in America than in any other country, yet the Welsh have nothing of the position in America that the Irish have. The primary factor is that American scholars have for some time recognized contemporary literature as a legitimate field for both criticism and research. The difference between America and Britain in this respect is very marked. In British universities, the general attitude—with a few fairly recent exceptions—tends to be that one does not, and does not need to, study academically one's own contemporary literature, which is part of the cultural world one lives in and which therefore one is supposed to absorb naturally; only the literature of the past, deriving as it does from a different background and posing special problems of understanding and interpretation, should be formally studied. This argument, of course, ignores the sheer difficulty of much twentieth century literature and the fact that a work of such a writer as Joyce has been shown to require the most careful explanation and interpretation in order to be properly available to the contemporary reader.

The whole problem of the difficulty, even the obscurity, of much modern literature is too complicated to be gone into here; it is part of the wider problem of the division of the audience for works of literature into highbrow, middlebrow, and lowbrow and the resultant movement of serious writers away from a popular audience; this in turn is bound up with the spread of literacy and the nature of modern popular education. (One of the reasons that contemporary literature is so widely studied in American colleges is a widespread view that what a young person reads *is only what he formally studies.* If the student is to read modern literature at all, therefore, he must read it in college classes.) But it is interesting that in America the difficulty of much modern literature has been used as a reason—or an excuse—for subjecting it to the heaviest kind of explanation and analysis. Joyce's complex verbal devices and Yeats's symbolism cry out for the analyst and the explicator, and they have not been slow in coming forward—just as the analysts and explicators of the poems and plays of T. S. Eliot have not hesitated to present themselves.

"Unity and Strife in Yeats' Tower Symbol," "A Liturgical Pattern in *Ulysses,*" "Thematic Development in T. S. Eliot's

'Hysteria' "—these are characteristic titles, picked at random from the *PMLA* bibliography for 1960. The last of these is worth considering briefly. Eliot's "Hysteria" is a prose poem (or a piece of prose description) about the reaction of an observer to a woman's laughter—the hysteria is more in the observer than in the woman. The poem is about a dozen lines long, is obviously an exercise in a certain kind of expression, and is neither very good, very interesting, nor very important. That someone should publish an article in *Twentieth Century Literature* solemnly analyzing the "thematic development" of this slight parergon is evidence not only of the classic stature that Eliot has achieved in America but also of the lack of sense of proportion in both scholars and editors in dealing with analytical articles.

About the problems posed by analytical articles in general I shall have something to say later. My immediate purpose is to indicate the popularity of twentieth century English literature as a field in which the American scholar may display himself. In every respect the American academics have dominated this field. They have produced surveys, anthologies, student aids and guides, bibliographies, editions, and compendiums covering the whole area; they have produced individual biographies and bibliographies, critical and explanatory studies, and annotated texts; and they have produced innumerable articles in learned journals and critical periodicals. How good are they? How far has this field been invaded by the fools and the freaks? How far has all this activity yielded centrally illuminating or at least genuinely helpful work?

Let us consider Yeats first. American work on Yeats is bewildering in its volume and diversity. The most generally

useful work on Yeats, which combines biography, explanation, description and interpretation of the significant poems,
and continuous discussion of the relation between Yeats's life,
thought, and work, seems to me to be *Yeats: The Man and
the Masks* by Richard Ellmann (1948). This is the book that
I recommend to students who want a sound and helpful introduction to a study of the poet. There is also *The Perma-
nence of Yeats* (1950), by two American academics—James
Hall and Martin Steinmann—who had the useful idea of
compiling an anthology of criticism of Yeats for the use of
students.[1]

Most of the significant work on Yeats in America has
been critical rather than scholarly. Edmund Wilson's discussion of Yeats in *Axel's Castle* (1931) was a pioneer study of
the poet's position in the modern literary movement, and in
the years since this appeared some of the most brilliant American critics have exercised their craft on Yeats's poems, notably the two Byzantium poems. R. P. Blackmur, Cleanth
Brooks, and Kenneth Burke are among those who have written detailed critical analyses of particular poems or discussed
critically some aspects of Yeats's technique. They were not always helped by the fact that the editions of the *Collected
Poems* published in New York often contained serious misprints. However, it was in considerable measure American
scholarship that remedied this, for the so-called *Variorum Edition of the Poems of W. B. Yeats* (1957) edited by Peter Allt

---

[1] This assembling within one volume of a collection of significant essays on a single great modern writer, primarily as an aid to students,
has been a characteristic American enterprise of the last decade or so.
There have been similar volumes on Joyce, *James Joyce: Two Decades of Criticism,* edited by Seon Givens (1948), and on Eliot, *T. S.
Eliot: A Selected Critique,* edited by Leonard Unger (1948).

13

and Russell K. Alspach was a joint enterprise by a young Anglo-Irishman who was killed in an accident in 1954 and an American scholar. This monumental work gives a full picture of Yeats's text, with all the variant readings of the different editions and revisions. Other scholarly and editorial work on Yeats—the editing of the letters, the writing of the life—has been left for the most part to Irish and English scholars; but the critical work done on Yeats in America is immensely larger in bulk than that done in Ireland or in Britain or indeed anywhere else.

Yeats has sometimes proved a dangerous subject for the bright analytical critic; his vocabulary is highly precise and linked to usages with which he was familiar and his symbolism is controlled by a quite specific pattern (or patterns) of thought. The English scholar F. A. C. Wilson has exposed the irrelevant fancifulness of some interpretations by showing, in two books on the background of Yeats's thought and the sources of his symbols (*W. B. Yeats and Tradition,* 1958, and *Yeats's Iconography,* 1960), exactly how the images and symbols were intended to work—though Wilson himself falls into the error of treating a poem of Yeats rather as though it were a simple coded message to be decoded by the scholar armed with the appropriate codebook. Perhaps the most notorious example of modern American critical interpretation erring through lack of understanding some of the basic linguistic elements involved is to be found in the article on Yeats by Delmore Schwartz that first appeared in the *Southern Review* in the winter of 1942 (VII, 3). Schwartz quotes (or misquotes) from the poem "Among School Children" the following lines.

Plato thought nature but a spume that plays
Upon a ghostly paradigm of things;
Soldier Aristotle played the taws
Upon the bottom of a king of kings;
World-famous golden-thighed Pythagoras
Fingered upon a fiddle-stick or strings
What a star sang and careless Muses heard:
Old clothes upon old sticks to scare a bird.

He comments:

Given the first two lines of the stanza, which are certainly
an effort to describe Plato's view of nature, suppose one takes
the next two lines as a description of Aristotle's cosmology.
"A king of kings" would thus be Aristotle's Prime Mover or
God; the taws or marbles would be the concentric spheres
which constitute the world for Aristotle and to which the
Prime Mover gives impetus or movement. The reference is
playful and ironic, and also exact in saying that the taws or
celestial spheres were played against the bottom of the Prime
Mover, since he is, in Aristotle's description of his life, turned
away from all nature and wholly engaged in eternal thought
about himself. . . . The succeeding four lines, as well as the
preceding two, help this interpretation by their reference to
Pythagoras on the same level of discourse, namely, different
philosophies of nature expressed in concrete figures. There is
nothing special to or limited to Aristotle about this interpretation of the two lines concerning him, for the Ptolemaic cosmology must be known in order to understand many other
authors [there follows a quotation of the last line of the *Di-*
vine Comedy as illustrating the same sort of thing]. . . .
Moreover, this interpretation seems to tally with what one
takes to be a misprint; "Soldier Aristotle" (which appears on

other areas where lack of knowledge distorts otherwise valuable American criticism and even scholarship.

The positive achievement in American work on Yeats is, however, very considerable indeed. It includes what is probably the best general study of the poet and his work; a number of extremely useful guides to the study of Yeats, intended for students, of a kind that cannot be found in any other country; and some splendid critical essays (notable among them R. P. Blackmur's two essays on Yeats in his *Language as Gesture*, 1952). The rapid establishment of Yeats as one of the great poets of the modern world and a classic of English literature is largely the result of the popularity of his work as a subject of academic study in the English departments of American universities and of the mass of writing about him that has partly produced and partly been produced by this popularity. As so often in this kind of academic popularity, there is both a gain and a loss. The gain is obvious; the loss results from the establishment of a "Yeats industry" (just as there is a "Joyce industry," a "Lawrence industry," and an industry for several other academically popular writers) that attracts the fools and the freaks and helps to encourage the view that a great writer exists simply as an object on which academic or critical teeth can be sharpened.

Significant American work on Joyce represents a larger proportion of all work done on that writer than is represented even by significant American work on Yeats. Richard Ellmann's thorough and definitive biography (*James Joyce*, 1959) is a work of long and patient scholarship that is absolutely invaluable to all students of Joyce. It is true that this is a different sort of biography from the kind that would be written on a writer long dead. Many of Joyce's friends, relatives, and acquaintances were alive when Ellmann was compiling his materials, and he was able to collect and preserve uniquely valuable biographical material by tape-recording their accounts of Joyce. It is perhaps easier to write this kind of biography than the more conventional kind, but it still involves an immense amount of labor and careful discrimination.

The two best introductions to Joyce and his work for both students and the general reader are by American scholars and critics—Harry Levin's *James Joyce: A Critical Introduction* (1941), the first book-length critical study of Joyce's whole achievement, and William York Tindall's *James Joyce* (1950). The first book devoted to a detailed interpretation of *Finnegans Wake* and still, in spite of the subsequent publication of much new work on the subject, a basic text for the study of Joyce is *A Skeleton Key to Finnegans Wake* by Joseph Campbell and Henry Morton Robinson (1944). The standard Joyce bibliography, by John J. Slocum and Herbert Cahoon, was published in 1953. The most comprehensive, if not the most consistently illuminating, book on Joyce is *Joyce: The Man, the Work, the Reputation* by Marvin Magalaner and Richard M. Kain (1956). The recovered portion of the first draft of *A Portrait of the Artist as a Young Man* was edited by Theodore Spencer and published in New York in 1944; a second edition, with additions, followed in 1955. Several of the stories from *Dubliners* have appeared in anthologies of the modern short story intended for college students, sometimes with careful critical analyses appended. Selections from *Ulysses* and *Finnegans Wake* appear in other college anthologies. Some 400 lines from *Finnegans Wake,* with some 9,000 words of explanation and annotation, appeared in *Modern Poetry: American and British* edited by Kimon Friar and John Malcolm Brinnin (1951). *Finnegans Wake,* probably the most explication-demanding work in the whole of English literature, has had a particular appeal for certain kinds of American critic. Thornton Wilder and William York Tindall have pursued the elusive meanings of this work, both alone and in study groups, for decades, and all over the country there are devotees who have made their own contribution.

In addition to full-length books (I have only mentioned a small proportion of these) and chapters of books, there are scores of articles on Joyce in the American critical reviews and learned journals. There is no sign of any decline in the amount of work being done on Joyce by American scholars and critics. In the issue of *PMLA* that reaches me as I write this chapter (June 1961) there is a long biographical article, "James Joyce: Unfacts, Fiction, and Facts," by William T. Noon, S.J., that goes carefully and helpfully into Joyce's attitude to the Jesuits and to Catholicism. (American Jesuits have naturally shown much interest in Joyce, whose schooling was at Jesuit institutions; sometimes they claim him as in spite of himself a true Catholic, sometimes they attack him, and sometimes again—as in the article just cited—they use their expert knowledge of Joyce's Catholic background to clear up disputed points.)

Looking through the immediately preceding numbers of *PMLA*, I find a 12,000-word article on a very slight and minor poem from Joyce's *Chamber Music* ("James Joyce's 'Tilly'" by Chester G. Anderson, LXXIII, 1958); a 16,000-word article examining the changes Joyce made over a period of fourteen years in a single sentence of *Finnegans Wake*

("From *Finnegans Wake:* A Sentence in Progress," by David Hayman, LXXIII, 1948); a 4,000-word article on Joyce's use of Aristotle's conception of modality ("The Modality of the Audible in Joyce's *Ulysses,*" by Joseph E. Duncan, LXXIII, 1957); and an article of less than 5,000 words on "Joyce's Use of Swift's *Polite Conversation* in the 'Circe' Episode of *Ulysses,*" by Mackie L. Jarrell (LXXII, 1957). The *James Joyce Review* has been appearing since February 1957. *Modern Fiction Studies* produced a special Joyce number in Spring 1958 (IV, 1), and in February 1952 the *CEA Critic* (College English Association) also devoted a special issue to Joyce. *A James Joyce Miscellany,* edited by Marvin Magalaner, first appeared in 1957; a second volume came out in 1959. There have been books published on *Joyce and Aquinas* (by William T. Noon, 1957), *Joyce and Shakespeare* (by William J. Schutte, 1957), *James Joyce and the Common Reader* (by W. Powell Jones, 1955), and on many other aspects of Joyce. Scholars and critics have discussed, in books or articles, Joyce and Mallarmé, Joyce and music, Joyce and Wagner, Joyce and Mozart, Joyce and the Elizabethans, Joyce and Ruskin, Joyce and Yeats, Joyce and Ibsen, Joyce and Rabelais, Joyce and Thomas Wolfe, Joyce and Sterne, Joyce and Alexandria, Joyce's criticism (which has been assembled and edited by Ellsworth Mason and Richard Ellmann, 1958), and almost any other aspect of Joyce one might care to name.

There are obvious dangers in this massive Joyce industry. Some of these are dangers involved in the pursuit of any detailed scholarship. Disproportion, the concentration on the trivial at the expense of the significant or on the irrelevant or marginally relevant at the expense of the central, is not confined to Joyce scholarship. It is an inevitable by-product of any large amount of scholarly activity in a single area and of any tradition of scholarship that emphasizes the importance of meticulously detailed research. This does not mean, of course, that there is anything wrong with such a tradition of scholarship, only that there is a necessary price one has to pay for it.

Further, what may appear trivial or irrelevant in one context may assume significance in another. If a writer is truly a great writer, then anything that may possibly illuminate his life and work may be of importance, and one can never predict what may turn out to be of importance. Nevertheless, there is a point beyond which lunatic scholarship begins. A study of the plans of a house in which Milton's father lived for a time before Milton was born cannot conceivably help us to understand Milton the poet or the man, and irrelevancies of this kind can be cited from among the work done on any major author, ancient or modern.

The special danger of work on Joyce, a writer whose deliberate exploitation by multiple puns of maximum associations of words and phrases presents a peculiar challenge to the explicator, is that any kind of ingenuity in explication can pass as helpful. I have seen a published analysis of a small section of *Finnegans Wake* that shows total ignorance of one of the main verbal references (a parody of "God Save the King") while pursuing every shadow of a possible allusion and bringing each one forward as a central meaning. A much acclaimed and more than once reprinted article on *Dubliners* argues with fantastic ingenuity that these stories follow events in the *Odyssey* in many respects more specifically and completely than the sections of *Ulysses* and that the whole

22

collection of stories is a kind of symbolic rewriting of the *Odyssey* ("First Flight to Ithaca: A New Reading of Joyce's *Dubliners*," by Richard Levin and Charles Shattuck, *Accent,* 1944). I myself am not convinced that this interpretation is anything more than a piece of misdirected ingenuity, and I believe that if the same effort were expended on almost any other work of English fiction one could find similar symbolic rewritings of the *Odyssey;* but whether one agrees with this interpretation or not one is (or ought to be) taken aback by the solemn implication that if this interpretation is valid, *so much the better.* My own view is that if this interpretation were valid it would mean that Joyce was acting as an obsessed crackpot in working into these stories of Dubliners crazy Homeric parallels that add nothing to the human meaning and reality of the stories and in fact, if taken into consideration, actually detract from their interest and value. The real danger, it would seem to me, of this sort of criticism is that there is absolutely no limit to what a critic can, by a desperate cleverness, "demonstrate" to be the meaning or meanings of a work or a part of a work, and that it is often deemed to be the duty of a younger member of an English department who seeks promotion to produce something of this kind, to pull out as many explicatory plums from the work as possible and exclaim triumphantly, "See what a good boy am I!"

Thus, together with much that is of the first importance in Joyce criticism, America has also produced too much solemn nonsense about Joyce. "Anything goes," once the industry is established and the rush for publication is under way. That splendid story "The Dead" (in *Dubliners*) can be presented as "a bitter parody of the events celebrated by the Roman

23

Catholic Church in its Epiphany Offices: the marriage at
Cana, the visit of the Magi, and the Baptism of Christ." This
piece of arrant nonsense is seriously argued in an article in
the Joyce number of *Modern Fiction Studies,* in this sort of
language:

> The marriage at Cana is represented in "The Dead" by the
> encounter of Gabriel with Lily, the caretaker's daughter.
> Gabriel gaily suggests that "we'll be going to your wedding
> one of these fine days with your young man, eh?"
> "The girl glanced back at him over her shoulder and said
> with great bitterness:
> " 'The men that is now is only all palaver and what they
> can out of you.' "
> Girls who cannot afford enough wine for the wedding do
> not usually get married at all in Joyce's Dublin. And Gabriel
> is reduced to consoling Lily for the loss of love by giving her
> a gold coin—a poor substitute for the turning of water into
> wine.
> The visit of the Magi to the Christ child and their shower-
> ing of gifts upon Him becomes the Misses Morkan's annual
> dance. Gabriel refers to the three hostesses as "the three
> Graces of the Dublin musical world" and praises them for
> their hospitality. But although they are genuinely kindly and
> hospitable, they are certainly not searching for a new revela-
> tion. Their name—Morkan—suggests that they are mawkins
> or spectres. They are the "three potatoes"—probably cold—
> which Lily reserves for Gabriel.

This is explication run mad; anyone who swallows this will
swallow anything.

On T. S. Eliot we can again distinguish really important
critical and scholarly work, dull pedestrian work that is helpful without being in any way brilliant, and the excesses of

freaks and fools. F. O. Matthiessen's *The Achievement of T. S. Eliot* (1935) was an important pioneer study of the poet that set the tone for a generation of Eliot criticism. Cleanth Brooks's analysis of *The Waste Land* in his *Modern Poetry and the Tradition* (1939) is the classic American explication of this long and difficult poem, which has had an enormous influence. George Williamson's *A Reader's Guide to T. S. Eliot: A Poem-by-Poem Analysis* (1953) is a learned and useful run-through of the poems that gives much helpful information without ever really indicating why the poems are worth all this trouble. Elizabeth Drew's *T. S. Eliot: The Design of His Poetry* (1950) is an interesting but sometimes rather labored description and explanation of the poems, with an emphasis on Jungian archetypes and a certain oversolemnity in dealing with the ironic and comic element in Eliot. (Thus Eliot's "Who clipped the lion's wings/ And flea'd his rump and pared his claws?" provokes the explanation that this is an "actualization into direct physical terms of diminution and decay.")

T. S. Eliot's Poetry and Plays: A Study in Sources and Meaning (1956) by Grover Smith Jr. is an elaborate, painstaking study, pretentious in manner and reverential in tone, packed with information and explanation, undeniably helpful, yet a terrible bore to read. Smith has a whole chapter on *Coriolan;* he tells us that Eliot "took a phrase or two from section 4 of Perse's Anabase and relied on Shakespeare's *Coriolanus* for some implicit historical background" and explains that "the supreme irony intrinsic to Eliot's use of Coriolanus as a symbol is that the Roman general stands for arrogant betrayal of people who also betray him," though he does not explain, what every reader of the poem wants to know, why Eliot

25

should use the quite un-Roman and un-English form of the name, Coriolan. Incidentally, it is amazing in what different things critics of Eliot can find "supreme irony"; the use of Coriolanus is doubtless ironical in Eliot's poems, but whether the simple point referred to by Smith constitutes *supreme* irony is certainly debatable.

There have been distinguished critical essays on Eliot by R. P. Blackmur, Francis Fergusson, John Crowe Ransom, J. J. Sweeney, Allen Tate, and Morton D. Zabel, among others. Even more than Joyce, Eliot has been anthologized and explicated in college anthologies. His position as a "culture hero" (in Delmore Schwartz's phrase) has been established in America now for some thirty years—to a greater extent, incidentally, than it has ever been in Britain. Though the number of articles on Eliot seems to be diminishing, much is still being written. There is, however, no *T. S. Eliot Review,* no *T. S. Eliot Newsletter* (so far as I am aware), and no annual *Eliot Miscellany.*

The other modern English writer whose study by American scholars and critics amounts almost to a cult is D. H. Lawrence; and here there *is* a *D. H. Lawrence News and Notes* run on cultist lines. Yet here also we find that some of the standard and central works on Lawrence are by Americans. It is interesting that in spite of the spate of reminiscent books about Lawrence by Englishmen and others who knew him, and two major English biographical and interpretative studies, it was left for an American scholar to find the patience and the determination to ferret out and organize in a cool objective narrative all the relevant facts about Lawrence's life. Upon publication, *The Intelligent Heart* (1955) by Harry T. Moore became at once the standard biography.

Another American, Edward Nehls, collected the biographical sources in three volumes that bring together all the available firsthand material (*D. H. Lawrence: A Composite Biography,* 1957-59). Harry T. Moore also edited, in 1948, Lawrence's letters to Bertrand Russell and is now engaged on a definitive edition of Lawrence's correspondence. The main work on Lawrence's bibliography has been done in America—by Edward D. Macdonald (*A Bibliography of the Writings of D. H. Lawrence,* 1925, and *The Writings of D. H. Lawrence, 1925-30: A Bibliographical Supplement,* 1931) and William White, whose checklist of Lawrence's publications from 1931 to 1950 (1950) is a further supplement to Macdonald's original volume. Maurice Beebe and Anthony Tommasi produced a "Selected Checklist" of the criticism of Lawrence "with an Index to Studies of Separate Works" in the Lawrence number of *Modern Fiction Studies* (V, 1959). (Similar checklists for other modern English and American novelists have appeared at intervals in *Modern Fiction Studies.*) *A D. H. Lawrence Miscellany* (1959), edited by Harry T. Moore, collected twenty-five essays on Lawrence by different hands, of very uneven quality. The fact that this collection appeared in the same year as the Lawrence issue of *Modern Fiction Studies* with its eight essays is an indication of how high Lawrence's reputation stood in 1959 and how attractive he was to American critics and scholars. Still, there is occasionally an air of scraping the bottom of the barrel in both collections; one gets tired of the perpetual symbol hunting in the novels and stories, though it is true that Lawrence did use objects and events as symbols and does therefore invite this kind of criticism.

One of the most interesting recent American contributions

to the study of Lawrence is the publication of texts that previously were not easily available. Lawrence's brilliantly idiosyncratic *Studies in Classic American Literature* was published as a paperback in 1953, and Harry T. Moore collected in one volume Lawrence's important fugitive pieces on *Sex, Literature, and Censorship* in 1955. There have been anthologies of Lawrence (as there have been of Joyce) and Lawrence's poetry and short stories have been well represented in college anthologies. Anthologists tend to copy one another's selections, however, and it is noticeable that "The Rocking Horse Winner"—not, perhaps, the best and certainly not the most characteristic of Lawrence's stories—is chosen again and again.

Lawrence was a prophet as well as a novelist and poet, with his own remedy for the ills of civilization, and this has involved an element in the appreciation of Lawrence that is not present in the appreciation of the other modern writers I have mentioned. Further, Lawrence in his lifetime was much attacked, often viciously and hysterically, and wilfully misrepresented. And finally, the question of censorship has come up with regard to his work to an even greater degree than to Joyce's. All this has given an air of personal commitment to a certain segment of the work done on Lawrence. While explicators of Eliot or Joyce, taking for granted the writer's greatness, content themselves with pointing out complexities of meaning or subtleties of allusion without demonstrating any personal excitement about Eliot's or Joyce's view of life (though there are some exceptions to this generalization), there is a tendency for commentators on Lawrence to defend as well as to explain him and sometimes to go further and join in the Lawrentian prophesying. Thus *D. H. Lawrence*

News and Notes is an organ of devoted Lawrentians who discuss their hero as though he were a religious leader, defend him against all comers (and on all issues), and write as though every relic of the great man were equally valuable. This has obviously produced a certain amount of silliness.

Looking at the whole field of American work on modern English writers, we can see an impressive picture. In the center are those works—bibliographical, biographical, and elucidatory—that have made available the relevant data and laid down general lines of interpretation. Beside these we must put those handbooks, study-aids, guides, annotated anthologies, and similar works that have played such an important part in making the works of these writers easily available and understandable. (One might add, however, that most of these works are written for college students, and the introduction of modern writers as topics for classroom study on a par with Shakespeare and Milton, rather than simply contemporary books to be read "for pleasure," argues a split between culture as a subject of formal instruction and culture as a part of daily living that has disturbing implications.) Then come the masses of articles, critical and scholarly; some develop a particular point about the writer's life, background, or thought, others present a detailed explication of a particular work or part of a work. Many of these articles are extremely valuable; even more are mildly interesting but not of any great significance; a minority—but still a considerable number—are unintelligent applications of a particular technique to inappropriate or irrelevant material or else the eccentric elaboration of preposterous ingenuities.

So far I have been considering work done on individual authors, but a striking feature of American scholarship on modern English literature has been the surveys of the whole field in the form either of literary history or of annotated anthologies. William York Tindall's *Forces in Modern British Literature* (1947) is a witty and provocative survey on English literature from about 1885, and as early as 1935 Fred B. Millett produced his *Contemporary British Literature: A Critical Survey and 232 Author-Bibliographies* which, while containing nothing critically original or exciting, was nevertheless a valuable aid to the study of the period up to the mid-1930's. Earlier still, Edmund Wilson's *Axel's Castle* (1931) presented pioneer studies of Yeats, Eliot, and Joyce among others, relating them to the whole European movement from the 1870's. Among anthologies, perhaps the most outstanding is *Modern Poetry: American and British,* edited by Kimon Friar and John Malcolm Brinnin (1951), which contains not only generous selections of poetry from Hopkins to Sidney Keyes but also some brilliant critical analyses of individual poems, notably Eliot's "Burnt Norton," *Ash-Wednesday, The Waste Land,* and "Gerontion," Yeats's Byzantium poems and "The Tower," and Dylan Thomas's "Vision and Prayer." (Yet it is perhaps indicative of the kind of simple factual mistakes about Britain that the most brilliant American critics of British poetry can make that in a note Isaac Rosenberg is said to have been born in Bristol, *Ireland.*)

An outstanding anthology with a limited chronological range, but showing a remarkable knowledge of the varieties of poetry produced throughout the British Isles in the decade from 1937 to 1947, is Kenneth Rexroth's *The New British Poets* (1948), whose introduction is the first critical essay by an American to take proper account of the poetry of the

Scottish Renaissance and is in general an important stock taking of the British poetic achievement from an immediately post-World War II vantage point. Louis Untermeyer's successively revised and enlarged editions of his *Modern British Poetry* (Mid-Century Edition, 1950) have kept track of critical fashion and made available to generations of college students selections of those modern British poets accepted by contemporary judgment as worth reading and teaching. His introductory accounts of each poet, while not notable for originality, are useful summaries of biographical fact and critical opinion. That indefatigable anthologist Oscar Williams has produced a popular anthology of modern poetry (*A Little Treasury of Modern Poetry*, 1946, with later revision) showing considerable breadth of knowledge and catholicity of taste. These are only a few examples of their kind; in the field of modern English literature as in other fields, the college anthology—more often than not accompanied by critical and explanatory notes—is a prominent and in some respects a unique American feature of the modern academic scene.

2

MILTON

Milton has long had a special place in American literary study, and has retained it in recent years in spite of the critical depreciation of him begun by Eliot and elaborated by F. R. Leavis. In fact, if not in the number of books and articles written then certainly in actual wordage, American work done on Milton is greater than almost any other area of scholarship. It is perhaps unfair to begin this summary by referring to Robert Adams' *Ikon: John Milton and the Modern Critics* (1955), a witty and sometimes malicious account of the extravagances of much modern Milton criticism and scholarship; yet in spite of exaggerations and suppressions, Adams' indictment has considerable justification. Some of the explicatory ingenuities offered by Cleanth Brooks and J. E. Hardy in their *Poems of Mr. John Milton* (1953) *are* preposterous; the archetypal and mythological approach to *Paradise Lost* of Arnold Stein (*Answerable Style,* 1953) and of R. J. Zwi Werblowsky (*Lucifer and Prometheus,* 1952) *can* result in confusion and exaggeration; the textual speculations in the third volume of Harris F. Fletcher's facsimile edition of *John Milton's Complete Poetical Works* (1948) and the whole "he-hee" edifice erected by Fletcher and others *do* verge on the absurd; the whole argument about Milton's rabbinical knowledge *has* been conducted by scholars insufficiently versed in the relevant rabbinical literature (Mr. Adams himself, it should be said, falls down here) and sometimes apparently unversed in the laws of evidence; and in general Milton's poetry *has* been almost sunk by the enormous weight of commentary of every conceivable kind that modern scholars and critics have loaded onto it. But obviously this is not the whole story.

A poet as learned as Milton, drawing so freely on all his resources of classical and Christian knowledge, a poet, moreover, who speaks as a Christian humanist to other Christian humanists who are expected to share the whole background of knowledge and ideas available to a seventeenth century left-wing Protestant scholar—such a poet surely demands that the modern reader make a conscious application of a carefully acquired background knowledge in order to ensure a correct reading. There is justification for the weight of scholarship attached to Milton in our time. In America, where classical learning is not likely to be part of the equipment of the student of English literature or indeed of any other kind of student, there is a special need to provide the relevant Latin and Greek references. The question is, of course, whether the references often provided are truly relevant and, further, whether the very lack of a tradition of classical knowledge among students and teachers does not make it easier for scholars to confuse the relevant and the irrelevant, the central with the peripheral, the plausible with the absurd.

One does not wish to stress unduly the modern decline of Latin and Greek learning in America, but the decline is an undisputed fact, and when one is discussing someone like Milton some account must be taken of it. (There are, of course, some distinguished exceptions, Douglas Bush, an able Latinist, being one.) I have recently seen an elementary mistake in Latin grammar in the translation of an easy Latin sentence in a newssheet written by and intended exclusively for American scholars, and again and again in works by American literary scholars one finds mistranslations from Latin or Greek, sometimes even schoolboy howlers. A Greek word whose sound is important to his argument is misspelled (and so mispronounced) in Robert Adams' *Ikon;* in the valuable facsimile edition of *Justa Edovardo King* (1939), the volume in which "Lycidas" first appeared, Ernest Mossner mistranscribes in his introduction the two Greek words on the title page, making an error in each by twice copying a *nu* as an *upsilon,* thus turning the phrase into total nonsense. I cite these two random examples because they came to my attention in books I have been looking at immediately before writing these pages.

Now, a certain law of compensation seems to operate where a particular kind of knowledge is in decline. Scholars lacking background in a special kind of knowledge and working on material that demands such knowledge will go very much further in providing scholarly apparatus, and parade a much wider area of scholarship, than will scholars whose backgrounds include such knowledge as part of every schoolboy's education. Where Macaulay's educated schoolboy would recognize an allusion to Virgil or Horace, the modern American scholar (sometimes missing the obvious allusion, or at least not realizing how more obvious and more central than others it is) will find a reference to scores of minor silver Latin works and to works far outside the whole field of Latin literature. It would be an exaggeration, and a most unfair one, to suggest that American Milton scholarship in general suffers from an overcompensation for the lack of a living tradition of classical scholarship among those working in English literature, but there is some element of truth in the charge. One might argue, of course, that it is not a "charge" at all, but a compliment. If scholars work unremittingly to expand their knowledge of a subject in which their education has hitherto been deficient and end up by knowing more about it than those who complacently assume that they know it all already, are they not to be congratulated? Yet it is not easy to compensate for lack of solid grounding in a language by piling up scholarly references. Such a piling up is subject to the law of diminishing returns: the more one finds, the less real use any part of it seems to be.

Having said this, one must go on to pay tribute to the remarkable achievement represented by modern American scholarship on Milton, to which the word *massive* seems fully appropriate. The assiduous biographical researches of J. Milton French range from the definitive account of Milton's financial affairs, *Milton in Chancery* (1939), to his five volumes of *Life Records of John Milton* (1949-58). James H. Hanford crowned a lifetime of Milton study with his biography of the poet, *John Milton, Englishman* (1949). The continuing researches in Milton's biography by William R. Parker have produced a number of important articles and are moving toward a great new biography. Milton's relation to the Puritan ideas of his day has been made thoroughly clear for the first time as a result of William Haller's two brilliant volumes on English Puritanism, the first of which, *The Rise of Puritanism* (1938), gives an account of the ideas expressed by Puritan preachers and writers from the time of the Elizabethan settlement to the time of the Long Parliament, and the second, *Liberty and Reformation in the Puritan Revolu-*

tion (1955), carries on the story from 1640 to 1649. Kester
Svendsen's *Milton and Science* (1956) reconsiders the much-
debated question of Milton's relation to the science of his time
and presents convincing evidence for modifying the traditional
answers. Milton's theology, especially as presented in his own
theological work *De Doctrina Christiana,* has been meticulously explained and analyzed by Maurice Kelley in *This Great
Argument* (1941). Howard Schultz's *Milton and Forbidden
Knowledge* (1955) gives a detailed account of attitudes to
different kinds of knowledge in the seventeenth century and
earlier—not all of them, it must be said, relevant to an understanding of Milton—thus enabling the student of Milton to
see the differences and the similarities between Milton's expressed views on this subject, from the First Prolusion to *Paradise Regained,* and the views available to him from tradition
or from contemporary currents of thought.

The books just mentioned represent a very small proportion indeed of the work done on Milton's life and thought,
but they are sufficient to indicate the range of biographical
inquiry, which is from the most minute investigation of do-
mestic circumstance to the relating of Milton's thought to his
reading and to the ideas prevalent during his time. The concern to set us right about Milton, to present this difficult and
still controversial figure as he really was, is evident in much
of this work, which often has an air of greater personal interest and commitment than the work done on other great
writers of the past. Douglas Bush, for example, gives his interpretation of Milton as a Christian humanist—in his *English Literature in the Earlier Seventeenth Century: 1600-
1660* (1945) and *Paradise Lost in Our Time* (1945)—with
the air of a man who feels it almost a moral need that we

should see Milton properly. It is surprising how Milton still comes home to men's business and bosoms.

In other work on Milton, however, we may find a kind of desperate comprehensiveness that pursues the most minute fact or document and seems to be motivated less by any interest in Milton's "real" significance as a poet and personality than by a determination to put everything in. It is perhaps significant that no American scholar or critic has produced a general account of Milton's life, work, and poetic achievement comparable to E. M. W. Tillyard's *Milton* (1930) or such a beautifully poised and rounded piece of scholarly investigation and presentation as F. T. Prince's *The Italian Element in Milton's Verse* (1954). The American Milton scholar does not as a rule deign to produce the kind of total picture that Tillyard aimed at; he is likely to be more interested in crossing other people's *t*'s and dotting their *i*'s or in discovering new facts or documents or allusions or possible influences or in making new interpretations of aspects of Milton's poetry or of his thought. American scholarship, which does so much for the student in the way of handbooks and anthologies, is not strong on general biocritical surveys of a writer, though it should be said that one of the best of such works, Joseph Wood Krutch's *Samuel Johnson* (1944), is an American product. This reluctance is probably related to the modern critical suspicion of general surveys and the preference for the analysis of the individual work; between the scholar intent on original research and the New Critic concerned with an ingenious new explication of a particular poem, the general biocritical study gets squeezed out. Or almost squeezed out—there are other examples than Krutch's book.

If we turn from work on Milton's life and thought to editions of his poetry and prose, we see a familiar fact—the American scholar's concern with making texts available to the student. The eighteen volumes of the Columbia Milton (1931-38), in the original spelling with full collations and an invaluable two-volume index (1940), or the vast Yale edition of the prose, still in progress, cannot compare in pedagogical usefulness or indeed in general serviceability with such editions as *The Student's Milton* edited by Frank A. Patterson (1930; revised edition, 1933), which collects in one volume all the poetry (in the original spelling), the greater part of the prose (including a translation of the *De Doctrina*), text and translations of the Italian, Latin, and Greek poems, early biographies of Milton, and an introduction and notes, or Merritt Y. Hughes's most generously and helpfully annotated *Complete Poems and Major Prose* (1957), or the annotated editions of the poems by James H. Hanford (1936; second edition, 1953) or Harris F. Fletcher (1941). These are readable volumes, with an apparatus that really helps the reader to fuller comprehension; their existence makes it possible to ensure that Milton is read, at least among students, and read with some understanding. In this sense Fletcher's "New Cambridge" edition of 1941 is a more useful work than his four-volume *John Milton, Complete Poetical Works, Reproduced in Photographic Facsimile* (1943-48), of which Robert Adams ironically remarks that it "carries reverence for the printed page to some sort of climax by reprinting both [the 1667 and the 1674] editions [of *Paradise Lost*] in facsimile and collating a great many copies of each." No doubt any serious student of Milton will on occasion have to look up the Columbia Milton, and no doubt also

38

he will at some time need the help of some one of the eight volumes of the Yale edition of the prose works (two volumes have so far appeared). It is necessary that scholarship should make available a complete and authoritative text of a great writer's total output; but it seems to me to be a more valuable achievement to have made some of Milton's lesser known prose available in a volume that can be bought and read than to have produced a huge library edition that will never leave the library. At any rate, one must pay tribute, in Milton studies as elsewhere, to the achievement of American scholars in making a wide range of Milton's work accessible to the non-specialist reader.

The Columbia Milton, though it appeared in the 1930's, was conceived much earlier. The originator of the idea was Professor W. P. Trent, who suggested it to President Butler of Columbia in 1908, the tercentenary year of Milton's birth. Trent had a reverence for Milton of a kind that modern Milton scholars would find embarrassing. "Shakespeare," he wrote in a little book on Milton published in 1899, "is the full blushing rose of human genius in its totality; Milton is the stately, pure, noble lily of human genius on its spiritual and ideal side." Trent persuaded Butler of the desirability of having Columbia sponsor the first complete edition of Milton's poetry and prose. The bulk of the work was done by scholars on the Columbia English faculty, whether they were originally Miltonists or not. Indeed, they became Miltonists in order to do their job—William Haller, who had done research on Southey, turned himself into a brilliant historian of Puritanism and Frank A. Patterson, who eventually carried most of the editorial load, moved from Wordsworth to Milton. Among those brought in from the outside to do specific jobs on the edition were James H. Hanford, J. Milton French, Alan Gilbert, and T. O. Mabbott, the last of whom was primarily a Poe scholar and who returned to Poe after his work on the edition was completed.

It is interesting that the Columbia edition was an exclusively Columbia enterprise (the Milton section of the Modern Language Association played no part in it except insofar as it provided a place in which Milton scholars could talk) and that a factor in this as in other large-scale undertakings was the ambition of an American university press to match the achievements of Oxford and Cambridge. The support provided by Frederick Coykendall (1882-1954), successively director of the Columbia University Press, president of its board, and chairman of the Columbia Board of Trustees, and a wealthy businessman and book collector, made possible the luxurious printing job. Whether the result really justified the energy and money spent on it remains a matter for argument. Preparation of the edition certainly generated an immense amount of scholarly activity, and it was something to have everything made available—although the miscellaneous material in Volume XVIII is, in Professor Hanford's words, "subject to infinite addition, subtraction, and correction." The price of the edition made it beyond the reach of the ordinary private purchaser, and I am told that copies are still available at the Columbia University Press.

Institutional pride and the kind of resources provided by the combination of donor, university press, and faculty concentrated on one campus, which operated to produce the Columbia Milton, had no place in the Yale Milton. In 1944, while teaching at New York University, Don M. Wolfe, author of *Milton in the Puritan Revolution* (1941) and *Leveller*

Manifestoes (1944), proposed a new edition of Milton's prose works to Yale University Press. One main aim was to remedy what scholars believed to be the two main defects of the Columbia edition: the absence of annotation (except for Volume XVIII); and the lack of chronological arrangement. The aim of the Yale Milton, as set forth in the preface to Volume I (1953) was "to present annotated texts of Milton's prose in the ascertainable order of its composition, bringing to bear in notes, prefaces, and volume introductions the accumulated scholarship of the past century." In 1948 an international and interuniversity editorial board was set up, consisting of Douglas Bush of Harvard, Alexander Witherspoon of Yale, Merritt Hughes of the University of Wisconsin, J. Milton French of Rutgers, Maurice Kelley of Princeton, A. S. P. Woodhouse of the University of Toronto, and Sir Herbert Grierson of Edinburgh University. The board thus brought together was able to enlist the aid of experts in various departments of Milton scholarship and history of ideas. With the recommendations and advice of Alvin Johnson, President Emeritus of the New School, and David Stevens, then of the Rockefeller Foundation, funds for publication were solicited from the Bollingen and Littauer Foundations. Volume II, edited by Ernest Sirluck, appeared in 1959.

The sheer amplitude of comment and annotation in the Yale edition has been found daunting by some readers, and while no one has quarrelled with the textual achievement (some textual problems have here been cleared up for the first time) there have been some objections made to the scope and detail of the introductions and notes. Douglas Bush, writing about the edition in *Renaissance News* (Autumn 1961) took note of these objections, but pointed out not only that the editors aimed at advancing knowledge and at critical reinterpretation as well as digesting and synthesizing previous scholarship, but also that "this edition is not offered solely to Miltonic and seventeenth-century experts; nor is it for people who prefer to read with half-knowledge or for those who do their reading in a library and don't mind jumping up every two minutes to look for works of reference." He added, fairly enough: "Annotation always runs the risk of excess, and no doubt this edition commits sins of that kind; but one can always skip a superfluous note while one cannot always supply a missing one." There may well be superfluities in these volumes, but they provide a storehouse of Milton scholarship and interpretation that exists nowhere else and that no serious student of Milton can afford to ignore.

Mention should also be made of the variorum notes to the poems, which are to be appended to the Columbia Milton. Much of the work for these volumes has already been completed but at the time of writing they have not yet appeared. Merritt Y. Hughes, who promoted the undertaking, is doing *Paradise Lost;* W. R. Parker, *Samson Agonistes;* Walter MacKellar, *Paradise Regained;* Douglas Bush, the Latin poems; and other scholars are concentrating on other parts of Milton's verse. The objective is to bring together comprehensively all that is valuable in comment on Milton's poetical work. Whether such an enterprise is really possible or valuable remains to be seen.

In the meantime, however, these three "monumental" works—the Columbia Milton, the Yale Milton's Prose, and the as yet unpublished Columbia variorum notes—stand out, and will for some time stand out, as some of the most spectacular achievements of literary scholarship in America, challenging comparison with such other monuments as the Manly-Rickert eight-volume edition of Chaucer's *Canterbury Tales* (1940), George Sherburn's five-volume edition of Pope's correspondence (1956), the fifty-odd volumes of Horace Walpole's correspondence edited by W. S. Lewis and others (1937 ff.), the ten volumes of Donne's sermons edited by George R. Potter and Evelyn M. Simpson (1953 ff.), and the thirty-odd volumes of Boswell papers edited by F. A. Pottle and others (1950 ff.).[1]

With the editions, one must mention the study-aids. Hanford's *A Milton Handbook* has gone through many editions since it was first published in 1926; it is precisely what it claims to be, a handbook; it lays out, with no trace of exhibitionism and a sober conservatism of mind, the facts about Milton's life, thought, and work that the student would want to know, and adds a bibliography. A study-aid with a more limited purpose, yet in some ways more exciting for the student, is represented by the collection of critical essays on "Lycidas" edited by C. A. Patrides (1961). This volume contains the 1645 text of the poem, with explanatory notes and a full collation, a reproduction of some of the corrections found in the Trinity manuscript, the "Epitaphium Damonis" followed by a translation, Hanford's essay on "The Pastoral Essay and Milton's 'Lycidas,'" twelve critical analyses of the poem from Dr. Johnson's to that of Brooks and Hardy (all but Johnson's are in fact modern), and a summing up and statement of his own position by M. H. Abrams, who also con-

[1] For information about the inception of the Columbia and Yale Miltons I am much indebted to private communications from Professor James H. Hanford and Professor Don M. Wolfe. I have also received helpful information from Professor Hanford about the origins of the New Humanism, which is discussed below.

tributes a foreword in which he points out the usefulness of the anthology equally "for courses in the history and theory of literary criticism and for courses in the introduction to literature, or in Milton, or in English poetry." The volume also includes a comprehensive bibliography.

This anthology, published relatively cheaply as a paperback, is a notable example of American enterprise in pedagogic helps. In studying adequately a poem like "Lycidas," Abrams says in his foreword, "hitherto the teacher has been thwarted by the need for the students to have simultaneous access to a great many books, some of them learned periodicals possessed only by large libraries and none of them in a sufficient number of copies to be practicable for any class larger than a small seminar." The present volume "makes available to each student the equivalent of a sizable shelf of books." The paperback anthology of critical essays is one of the latest and most exciting of the devices invented by American scholars and critics for increasing the availability of texts. Others of these anthologies include: *Chaucer: Modern Essays in Criticism,* edited by Edward Wagenknecht (1959); *Tragic Themes in Western Literature,* edited with an introduction by Cleanth Brooks (1955); *Eighteenth Century English Literature: Modern Essays in Criticism,* edited by M. H. Abrams (1960); and *Victorian Literature: Modern Essays in Criticism,* edited by Austin Wright (1961).

So on the one hand we have the Yale prose volumes, with their vast quantity of bibliographical, textual, biographical, historical, and topical information, and on the other we have the compact portable anthology in which scholarship and criticism from a great diversity of sources have been brought together for the convenience of the student or the general reader. These two extremes illustrate two opposing drives in modern American academic life—to produce an uncompromisingly scholarly work packed with detailed annotation, the result of minute and long-continued original scholarship, and to facilitate the serious study of literature in colleges by making the results of scholarship and criticism, as well as the texts themselves, easily available. One may perhaps be permitted to assume the presence somewhere here of a third party in addition to the student and the teacher. This is the publisher, increasingly aware of the ever growing number of students in colleges and of the need for texts and eager to cooperate in any enterprise that will result in the sale of large numbers of his publications. Hard things have been said, often with justice, about publishers, but it is only proper to record that in this matter of making texts easily available to students publishers' self-interest works in the best interests of education and (but in *this* matter only) American publishers have the best record of any publishers in the world. The whole question of the "paperback revolution" and its significance for American literary education is discussed in a later section.

If one leaves biographical and editorial work on Milton to give some picture of the general critical work on the poet, one very rapidly loses one's bearings, for the variety and the varying quality of interpretative and critical studies of Milton's poetry are positively bewildering. One might begin by setting side by side the Brooks-Hardy analyses of Milton's minor poems, already referred to, and Rosamund Tuve's *Images and Themes in Five Poems by Milton* (1957). Miss Tuve is concerned to interpret the poems in the light of the literary and rhetorical traditions in which they were written and of which the author was aware; just as she reproves Empson for his unhistorical reading of George Herbert, so she reproves Brooks and Hardy for a similar irresponsibility. One might take a middle position and argue that one's interpretation of a poem need not be limited by the application of the rules of the relevant genre as known and practiced in the author's time (poets, least of all great poets, do not write to rule) while at the same time showing uneasiness at what Abrams calls the "notable sleight of explication" by which Brooks and Hardy turn "Lycidas" into a modern symbolist poem.

Some modern critical analyses of poems of Milton seem to be exercises in explicatory ingenuity in which the aim appears to be to demonstrate just how far the critic can go in reading into the poem a complex pattern of imagery while ignoring not only the ostensible subject and the implications of the genre but all indications of tone, mood, and emphasis provided by rhythmic and other aural devices. But even these excesses, if their method is not unduly mechanical (as it sometimes is), keep the issue alive and provoke further argument and discussion. It is interesting that the anti-Miltonist position adumbrated by Eliot in his essay on the metaphysical poets (1921), developed in his essay on Milton (1936), and elaborated by F. R. Leavis (*Revaluation,* 1936), which has caused so much pro and con Milton controversy in England, has not been a topic of much discussion in America. The American New Critics who have turned to Milton have, on the whole, seen his poems as objects on which to exhibit their analytic and explicatory skills (the implicit assumption being that any poem to which such skills are applicable is good) rather than as awful examples of lack of a visual imagination and excessive book learning.

Studies of *Paradise Lost* range from a placing of Milton's treatment of the story of the creation among the treatments by theological commentators on Genesis (*Milton's Paradise with Reference to the Hexameral Background,* by Sister Mary Corcoran, 1945) to Arnold Stein's *Answerable Style* (1953), which reaches Milton's thought through a study of his poetic imagery with a somewhat unanchored brilliance. Don C. Allen's *The Harmonious Vision* (1954) is another work that approaches Milton's imagination through a study of his imagery, and is, incidentally, one of the few American studies that directly confront and reduce to size the view of Eliot and others that Milton lacked a proper visual imagination. Elizabeth M. Pope's *Paradise Regained: The Tradition and the Poem* (1947) is a carefully executed study of the relation of Milton's treatment of the temptation of Christ by Satan to traditional handlings of the theme and genuinely illuminates the poem; F. M. Krouse's *Milton's Samson and the Christian Tradition* (1949) does something similar for *Samson Agonistes.* W. R. Parker's *Milton's Debt to Greek Tragedy in Samson Agonistes* (1937) is a definitive treatment of its subject, and, like all Parker's work on Milton, it is marked by thoroughness, relevance, and an intelligent conservatism of approach.

This is but to skim the surface of American Milton scholarship; my sketch makes no claim to completeness and many distinguished names go unrecorded. The aim of these few paragraphs is simply to adumbrate the lines on which American Milton scholarship and criticism has been proceeding. And it still proceeds. Over fifty items on Milton (books and articles) were published by American scholars in 1950, ranging from J. Max Patrick's *Milton's Conception of Sin as*

Developed in "Paradise Lost" to George R. Waggoner's article on "The Challenge to Single Combat in Samson Agonistes" in the *Philological Quarterly.* For a general defense of American Milton scholarship, the reader is referred to Don M. Wolfe's article, "Milton Under Glass," which appeared in the (London) *Times Literary Supplement* of 18 May 1956. Though the record includes a considerable amount of scholarly hair-splitting and critical extravagance, it is nevertheless a noble one. While it might be true to say that no single American work on Milton presents that total revaluation of the poet and his achievement that is still a desideratum, it can be said most emphatically that American scholarship has made such a comprehensive study possible by making available in abundant detail all the relevant (as well as some irrelevant) material. One might indeed venture a generalization about American literary scholarship: whatever its limitations in the field of general revaluation, it provides, by its industry, its thoroughness, and its intellectual strenuousness, the basic facts and ideas on which any comprehensive reinterpretation must depend.[2]

[2] An excellent example of this occurred after this section was written. William Empson's original reinterpretation of *Paradise Lost* and *Samson* (*Milton's God,* 1961) is a strikingly provocative study that, while wholly original in its point of view and in many of its conclusions, draws heavily on American research in deploying its arguments.

3

SHAKESPEARE

The enormous volume of work produced by American scholars and critics on Shakespeare during the last thirty years has
included, in addition to special studies on almost every conceivable aspect of the dramatist, a number of valuable general surveys of the Shakespearean achievement; in this respect
American Shakespeare studies differ from Milton studies,
which, as has been noted, have produced no comprehensive
reappraisal of the poet's work. Of these, Theodore Spencer's
Shakespeare and the Nature of Man (1942), Mark Van Doren's *Shakespeare* (1939), Hardin Craig's *An Interpretation
of Shakespeare* (1948), and H. G. Goddard's *The Meaning
of Shakespeare* (1951) are the most interesting. In *The
Meaning of Shakespeare* a certain amateurishness and even
rashness are offset by the author's engaging desire to make
manifest his interest and enthusiasm, a wide range of reference, and a broad humanist curiosity—none of these qualities
being especially conspicuous in modern American academic
literary scholarship.

There have also been some significant American contributions to the interpretation of the thought and imagination of
the whole Elizabethan period. Hardin Craig's *The Enchanted
Glass: The Elizabethan Mind in Literature* (1936) has
achieved almost classic status, while Douglas Bush's *Mythology and the Renaissance Tradition* (1932) and *The Renaissance and English Humanism* (1939), Rosamund Tuve's

49

Elizabethan and Metaphysical Imagery (1947), Lawrence Babb's *The Elizabethan Malady: A Study of Melancholia in English Literature from 1580 to 1642* (1951), and Madeleine Doran's *Endeavors of Art: A Study of Form in Elizabethan Drama* (1953) deal with particular aspects of the literature of the period from a wide perspective. These items are culled from a far greater number simply because I have had occasion to draw on them myself, in trying to increase my understanding of Elizabethan and Jacobean literature, and have found them extremely helpful.

Once again we have to notice the American scholar's (and publisher's) interest in making texts and interpretations available. The college teacher has a wide choice of texts. Thomas M. Parrot's *Shakespeare: Twenty-Three Plays and the Sonnets* (1938) includes as an introduction the whole of the editor's previously published *William Shakespeare: A Handbook* (1934) as well as providing introductions and notes to each play; Holzknecht and McClure's attractively presented four volumes of *Selected Plays of Shakespeare* (1937-41) lack the large general introduction of Parrot's edition but have introductions and notes to the plays. A complete one-volume edition of Shakespeare with introduction and notes (1942), edited by William A. Neilson and Charles J. Hill, was based on Neilson's Cambridge Edition of 1906, with much revision of both text and apparatus. Another great scholar of an older generation, G. L. Kittredge, produced a complete one-volume edition of Shakespeare in 1936, as well as a volume of sixteen plays published in 1946 and separate editions of individual plays. The forty volumes of the Yale Shakespeare (1918-28) edited by Wilbur L. Cross, C. F. Tucker Brooke, and others, came before the period with which

I am concerned, but this college edition not only indicates the continuity of the tradition, but is itself now being made available (as revised under the general editorship of Helge Kökeritz and Charles T. Prouty) in paperback volumes.

The pioneer paperback Shakespeare, begun in 1937 and recently completed, is the Penguin Shakespeare, edited by G. B. Harrison; though the publishers are English the editor is a distinguished American (if ex-English) Shakespeare scholar. The Pelican Shakespeare (1946 ff.) under the general direction of Alfred Harbage, of which eleven volumes have appeared to date, is another popular paperback series of the individual plays, each edited by a notable scholar: Matthew W. Black's *Richard II,* Matthew A. Shaaber's *I Henry IV,* Louis B. Wright and Virginia Freund's *Henry V,* Alfred Harbage's *Macbeth,* and R. C. Bald's *Measure for Measure* are some of the earlier examples of this well-edited and easy-to-handle edition, each volume of which has an introductory essay by Harbage on "Shakespeare and his Stage" as well as an introduction to the play by the special editor and notes at the foot of the page. The Folger Library General Reader's Shakespeare (1957 ff.) is another popular paperback series recently begun, with Louis B. Wright and Virginia Freund editing some of the volumes and Wright and Virginia A. LaMar doing others. The introductory material to each contains a life of Shakespeare, an account of his stage, a discussion of the particular play, "references for further reading," and a generous number of reproductions illustrating the background (excessively reduced, however, because of the smallness of the page). The printing of the notes ("as brief and simple as possible") on the pages facing the text makes for ease of reading and leaves space for further notes by the student. Yet another paperback Shakespeare collection with a volume to a play is the Laurel Shakespeare under the general editorship of Francis Fergusson (1960 ff.) of which fifteen volumes have appeared at the time of writing. Commentaries are supplied by actors, directors, or dramatic critics (occasionally by a Shakespeare scholar—e.g., D. A. Traversi does *The Winter's Tale*) who include Margaret Webster (*The Taming of the Shrew*), Flora Robson (*Macbeth*), and Maurice Evans (*Hamlet*). W. H. Auden writes on *Romeo and Juliet.* The general editor supplies a short introduction on each play and also an essay on "Shakespeare and His Theatre" that is printed at the end of each volume. The text is that of C. J. Sisson. The facsimile of the First Folio edited by Helge Kökeritz and Charles T. Prouty (1955) gives the student the opportunity of seeing for himself what the text of the plays looked like in their first collected edition. Leonard F. Dean has edited *Shakespeare: Modern Essays in Criticism* (1957) thus making easily available to the student a wide range of modern critical essays.

While it is important, here as elsewhere, to note the great amount of work done in making Shakespeare available and fully intelligible to the student (and perhaps to the general public also—presumably the paperbacks are aimed at the widest possible readership; but I should still guess that the readers are mostly students), the fact remains that the most characteristic American contributions to Shakespeare studies run on more specialized lines.

The New Variorum Edition, begun in 1871 and still in progress, is the fullest of all editions, with a massively annotated volume to each play; it was certainly never meant for the general reader. Each volume assembles almost everything known and written about and everything possibly relevant to each play as well, of course, as presenting the best text that contemporary scholarship can produce. It is in the textual aspect that the very scale of the enterprise tends to defeat itself, for while it takes years to complete a volume, knowledge and understanding of Shakespeare's text has been for many years leaping ahead annually, and there is still a lot more to learn. The result is that in some important respects a New Variorum volume may be out of date as soon as it is published.

Consider for example the case of the New Variorum of *Troilus and Cressida* (1953). This was begun by H. N. Hildebrand and completed and seen through the press by T. W. Baldwin, who added some material of as late as 1951. But he did not include the significant new textual discoveries about *Troilus* even though these had in fact been made available by Alice Walker ("The Textual Problem of *Troilus and Cressida*," *MLR,* XLV, 1950) and Philip Williams ("Shakespeare's *Troilus and Cressida:* The Relationship of Quarto and Folio," *Studies in Bibliography,* 1950), working independently. The printer of the Folio was held up by some obstacle after printing three pages of *Troilus and Cressida,* and while waiting for a solution to his difficulty (which was eventually found) he was able to get hold of the Quarto text of the play into which superior readings had been copied, so that when printing of *Troilus* was resumed, he printed from this marked copy of the Quarto and not (as he had done for the first three pages) from an uncorrected Quarto text. Any discussion of the Folio text of *Troilus* that ignores this discovery is bound to be inadequate.

The New Variorum Edition thus has a tendency to sink

with its own weight; it is nevertheless an invaluable scholarly enterprise. Begun by Horace Howard Furness and continued by his son and namesake, it was transferred to the auspices of the Modern Language Association of America in 1936. It was in that year that the New Variorum of *I Henry IV* appeared, an edition out of date in many respects by the mid-1950's, with the result that the Shakespeare Association of America commissioned a supplement that appeared in 1956 (*Supplement to Henry IV, Part I, A New Variorum Edition,* edited by G. Blakemore Evans) and printed "with some degree of completeness all (mere nonsense aside) that has been written relating to the play from 1935 to 1955." The *Supplement* has been described as "all notes and no text—the pedant's dream" and also (by the same reviewer) as containing what teachers of Shakespeare "simply have to know."

This is indeed a sobering thought, and if the Shakespeare Association of America goes ahead with its tentative plans of publishing supplements to other New Variorum volumes, one has visions of teachers of Shakespeare continually pursuing these supplements in a vain attempt to catch up with what they "simply have to know." But the thought of their being without such aids is even more sobering. It is in fact humanly impossible for any individual to master all the scholarly and critical material on Shakespeare that is now being brought out annually. Even if one confined oneself to American material alone, one would find it almost a full-time job. Meanwhile one can contemplate the paradox that a truly comprehensive volume on even a single play of Shakespeare is bound to take so long to produce that it will inevitably be out of date when it appears, while one that can be produced quickly enough to be abreast of all recent developments will not have space enough to take account of them all.

Of course, one of the chief reasons for the great amount of material written about Shakespeare is the depth and complexity of his plays and the continual challenge that they present. There will never be a "definitive" interpretation of Shakespeare, and each generation will continue to explain him in its own way and to concentrate on those aspects of his work that it finds most interesting and revealing.

One strand of modern Shakespeare scholarship has tried to see Shakespeare in the light of the dramatic and artistic conventions of his time and to define the limits of interpretation with reference to such conventions. Elmer E. Stoll was a pioneer in emphasizing the importance of dramatic artifice in building up the necessary illusion; in *Art and Artifice in Shakespeare* (1933) as well as in other of his many volumes of Shakespeare criticism, he attacked the Bradleyan approach to the characters in Shakespeare's plays, which considered them as self-contained characters in psychologically realistic terms, and saw the characters as existing merely in terms of the impressions about them produced by the author at given moments in the play, so that questions of consistency or contradiction do not arise. There has perhaps been an overemphasis by some American scholars on Shakespeare's dependence on the conventions and ideas of his day, but a salutary mitigation of romantic extravagance in the light of sober scholarship (and Stoll's drawing attention back to the play and how it works as a play was certainly salutary) can itself become an extravagance. To be told, as we are by some more recent writers, that certain admired or puzzling effects in

Shakespeare are there "because" of a certain tradition or of the existence of certain prototypes of particular characters is often to be told very much less than the writer imagines.

Nevertheless, understanding has certainly been advanced by a greater number of significant American studies in Shakespeare in relation to his background than can possibly be mentioned in a survey of this kind. Lily B. Campbell's *Shakespeare's "Histories": Mirrors of Elizabethan Policy* (1947) relates, with abundant and even ponderous scholarship, Shakespeare's history plays to Elizabethan thinking about the uses of history and its relation to politics. T. W. Baldwin, in *Shakspere's Five-Act Structure* (1947), examines the significance for Shakespeare of the Renaissance traditions (derived from commentators on Terence) of act-division. Oscar J. Campbell's *Comical Satyre and Shakespeare's "Troilus and Cressida"* (1938) and *Shakespeare's Satire* (1943) relate particular phases of Shakespearean drama to certain contemporary conditions. Although he makes some illuminating points, Campbell does tend to over-emphasize possible historical analogies and explanations without sufficiently attending to what the plays, with all their richness and complexity of expression and structure, are actually saying. Sister Miriam Joseph's *Shakespeare's Use of the Arts of Language* (1947) examines in the utmost detail the background and development of Elizabethan theories of the art of composition and, on the assumption that Shakespeare like other Elizabethan schoolboys had been taught rhetoric and composition according to these theories at school, traces their influence in his work. Again, one feels that some extremely interesting and illuminating historical material is being pressed to account for more than is perhaps reasonable.

Willard Farnham's *The Mediaeval Heritage of Elizabethan Tragedy* (1936) investigates some medieval elements in Shakespeare's plays; a less purely historical approach is shown in the same author's *Shakespeare's Tragic Frontier* (1950), where paradoxes in the characters of some of Shakespeare's later tragic heroes are related to parallels in the literature of the beginning of the seventeenth century. Another interesting attempt to explain a Shakespeare character with reference to the background of the time is J. W. Draper's *The Hamlet of Shakespeare's Audience* (1938). Alfred Harbage's *Shakespeare and the Rival Traditions* (1952) examines the significance for Shakespeare's dramatic development of the split (both in audience and in outlook) between the public and the private theatre, the first truly national and deriving from sources bound up with vital popular traditions, and the second a coterie theatre with academic and courtly sources. Harbage has also produced, in *As They Liked It: A Study of Shakespeare's Moral Artistry* (1947), a deservedly popular short book on the ways in which Shakespeare worked moral implications into his plays.

W. G. Meader, in *Courtship in Shakespeare: In Relation to the Tradition of Courtly Love* (1954), handles historical material with less deftness and provides an example of an oversimplified thesis pressed on recalcitrant facts. There is always the danger of the enthusiast being carried away by his own idea or discovery and pushing beyond reason. Roy Battenhouse sees Shakespeare's view as essentially Christian and in "Shakespearean Tragedy: A Christian Interpretation" (*The Tragic Vision and the Christian Faith,* ed. N. A. Scott Jr., 1957) argues for the Christian meaning of Shakespearean tragedy, while Sylvan Barnet inveighs against critics who try

57

to interpret Shakespeare in Christian terms ("Some Limitations of a Christian Approach to Shakespeare," *ELH*, XXII, 1955). J. W. Draper's *The Humors and Shakespeare's Characters* (1945) uses Elizabethan psychology to explain aspects of Shakespeare's character drawing, while Louise C. Turner Forest warns against depending too much on an oversimplified view of what Elizabethan psychology in fact was ("A Caveat for Critics Against Invoking Elizabethan Psychology," *PMLA*, LXI, 1946). Abbie Findlay Potts tries to show that after 1600 Shakespeare drew on Spenser to give ethical meaning to his plays (*Shakespeare and the Faerie Queene*, 1958) and makes an elaborate case for a thesis that remains for most readers quite unacceptable. C. L. Barber, in *Shakespeare's Festive Comedy* (1959), relates Shakespearean comedy to traditions deriving from the old folk festivals; like so many studies of this kind it illuminates without telling the whole story.

The partial vision of the scholar with a thesis is not to be despised; it is often the only way a body of knowledge and understanding can be built up; nevertheless, it remains *partial* and must not be mistaken for the whole truth. Scholars often find the passion for writing about their partial visions only by pretending that they are not partial but total. This is an inevitable element in scholarship that is by no means confined to American or Shakespeare studies; however, because Shakespeare studies are so diverse and so abundant it is an element easily found among them.

A brilliant example of a great Shakespeare sleuth who has made many invaluable discoveries but who is prone to push generalizations from them further than is reasonable is Leslie Hotson, whose discovery of the record of the inquest on Marlowe (*The Death of Christopher Marlowe*, 1925) was one of the most exciting scholarly events of the 1920's. His contributions to Shakespeare biography and to our understanding of Shakespeare's relation to Elizabethan customs and traditions (*Shakespeare Versus Shallow*, 1931; *I, William Shakespeare, Do Appoint Thomas Russell Esquire . . .* , 1937; *Shakespeare's Sonnets Dated and Other Essays*, 1949; *Shakespeare's Motley*, 1952) are all full of fascinating information drawn from original sources, but in some of these books he tends to draw conclusions not wholly justified by the information he provides. His study of Shakespeare's theatre (*Shakespeare's Wooden O*, 1959) and his learned and provocative *The First Night of Twelfth Night* (1954) show the same tendency to draw more confident conclusions than the evidence seems to warrant. Hotson is one of the few American Shakespeare scholars of whom it might be said that in his books he aims at the gallery; but this gives his writing a zest and a liveliness lacking in most of his colleagues. He is in many respects a unique phenomenon in the American scholarly scene, and thus deserves a paragraph to himself.

A great deal of patient work on Shakespeare biography has been done by American scholars. B. R. Lewis produced *The Shakespeare Documents: Facsimiles, Transliterations, Translations, and Commentary* (2 vols., 1940). T. W. Baldwin has studied Shakespeare's education in two important books (*Shakespere's Petty School*, 1943; *Shakespere's Small Latine and Lesse Greeke*, 2 vols., 1944); John Henry de Groot has most carefully considered the evidence that Shakespeare's parents were Roman Catholics (*The Shakespeares and the Old Faith*, 1946); Alan Meen and Robert Lubbock persuaded themselves that they saw Shakespeare's hand and mind

59

at work in the annotations discovered in a copy of Hall's *Chronicle* (*The Annotator,* 1954); Harold G. McCurdy ventured, somewhat rashly, on a modern psychological portrait of the dramatist (*The Personality of Shakespeare,* 1953); J. G. McManaway has discussed and published important Shakespeare documents and has written a valuable essay putting together the latest information about the order in which Shakespeare wrote his plays ("Recent Studies in Shakespeare's Chronology," *Shakespeare Survey,* III, 1950). Guess work and special pleading exist side by side with the sober products of industry, patience, and caution. The total contribution is considerable.

Modern critical preoccupation with the differentiating qualities of the poetic use of language has produced, predictably, a great crop of discussions of Shakespeare's imagery and of his use of language generally. Standing apart from these, and treating with a fine scholarly thoroughness an aspect of Shakespeare's language that has too little attention, is *Shakespeare's Pronunciation* by Helge Kökeritz (1953). A more characteristic American interest—the significance of Shakespeare's imagery for the total meaning of the given play—is explored in Robert B. Heilman's *The Great Stage: Image and Structure in "King Lear"* (1948), perhaps the most sustained and carefully wrought example of the investigation of the function of imagery and its relation to dramatic structure in all modern Shakespeare criticism. The dangers and limitations of this approach were demonstrated by W. R. Keast in his brilliant if savage discussion of Heilman's book ("The New Criticism and *King Lear," Modern Philology,* XLVII, 1949). The English Institute devoted one of its annual conferences to what has been called the "myth and metaphor" approach to Shakespeare among other writers and in *English Institute Essays, 1948* (1949) printed the four Shakespeare papers together under the title *Myth in the Later Plays of Shakespeare.* Among these is Heilman's essay "The Lear World," a bold and interesting interpretation that sees in *Lear* the evil workings of a purely rational approach to life when no longer given meaning by the ordering myths of governance and of love.

The "myth and metaphor" approach derives in some degree from the work of the English Shakespeare critic G. Wilson Knight, but American critics have developed this trend in their own way, sometimes with impressive originality, sometimes with fantastic absurdity. When we get an interpretation of *The Winter's Tale* as straight allegory, with Hermione representing Christ, Leontes the Jews, Mamilius the Jewish Church, and Perdita the Christian Church ("Shakespeare's Allegory: *The Winter's Tale,*" by J. A. Bryant Jr., *Sewanee Review,* LXIII, 1955) the line that separates the ingenious from the ridiculous has been crossed. We might contrast Elizabeth Pope's interpretation of *Measure for Measure* ("The Renaissance Background of *Measure for Measure,*" *Shakespeare Survey,* XI, 1958), which is controlled by a use of the history of ideas. Between these two extremes—interpreting Shakespeare in the light of Elizabethan ideas and interpreting him in the light of the critic's uncontrolled ingenuity—almost every gradation is to be found in modern American Shakespeare criticism.

Much useful work has been done by American scholars on Shakespeare's and the Shakespearean stage. *The Globe Playhouse: Its Design and Equipment* (1942) by J. C. Adams developed a view that has not found general acceptance though it stimulated much fruitful controversy. G. R. Kernodle's *From Art to Theatre: Form and Convention in the Renaissance* (1944), Leslie Hotson's *The First Night of Twelfth Night,* and Irwin Smith's *Shakespeare's Globe Playhouse: A Modern Reconstruction* (1956) are among the most significant works in this field. Smith's book on the whole follows Adams (in this respect not being typical of recent scholarship), but it also gives a full account of the results of modern research on the subject. Charles T. Prouty's "An Elizabethan Playhouse" (*Shakespeare Survey,* VI, 1953) ingeniously investigates the churchwardens' accounts of St. Botolph without Aldersgate from 1557 to 1568, finding receipts for the rental of Trinity Hall by players and thus throwing light on the development of the Elizabethan playhouse. American scholars have shown in many fields considerable imagination in seeking new kinds of documentary evidence that had not hitherto been considered relevant but that when properly interpreted can be made to yield really useful information. In this particular kind of enterprise American scholarship is probably ahead of that of any other country.

There is another field, too, in which one turns to American scholars for the industry, the patience, and the long-term planning that used to be characteristic of a certain kind of English scholarship (e.g., the Herford and Simpson eleven-volume edition of Ben Jonson, 1925-52, and E. K. Chambers' *The Elizabethan Stage,* 4 vols., 1923) but that are not easily found now in England. G. E. Bentley's *The Jacobean and Caroline Stage* (5 vols., 1941-56) continues Chambers' classic survey of every aspect of the Elizabethan theatre—the plays, the playwrights, the players, the theatres and the conditions under which they operated—into the Jacobean period.

Bentley's work, which for meticulous accuracy of detail and comprehensiveness of coverage outdoes Chambers', is in turn now a classic study. It is a work of reference rather than one to be read through, an indispensable guide for anyone working seriously on Jacobean or Caroline drama.

Finally, there is the field of textual studies, where American scholarship has in recent years made advances that have turned the whole subject into a specialist science that somewhat bewilders the layman. The establishment of bibliography and textual criticism as indispensable tools for the editor, and indeed for the literary scholar in general, was the work of three great English scholars, A. H. Pollard, W. W. Greg, and R. B. McKerrow. In the early years of the present century Greg and McKerrow laid down new standards of knowledge and accuracy in textual criticism, principally of Elizabethan texts. Greg's ferocious if often deserved reviews of the work of editors that showed no understanding of the kind of precise textual knowledge needed by an editor helped to change the whole face of English editing, while McKerrow's edition of Nashe (5 vols., 1904-10) provides an impressive example of how a modern editor ought to proceed. The foundation of the Bibliographical Society (London) and its periodical, *The Library* (1889 ff.), provided a forum for bibliographical and textual studies, and the new science grew rapidly with the twentieth century. J. Dover Wilson's New Cambridge edition of Shakespeare (1921 ff.) made increasing use of the new textual criticism and familiarized new generations of students with its procedures by the discussion of the nature of the copy-text that Wilson included in the volume devoted to each play. For *Hamlet,* there is a special two-volume study devoted to the textual problems (*The*

Manuscript of Shakespeare's Hamlet and the Problems of Its Transmission, 1934).

The main problem with which modern critical bibliography and textual criticism concerns itself is the understanding of the processes that take place between the manuscript's leaving the author's hands and the appearance of the printed book. Such understanding permits the reconstruction of the text as originally written by the author from the printed text with as much certainty as possible. The probable relation of the printed "original" to the author's manuscript is thus the primary topic of investigation; in order to pursue this an editor requires a detailed understanding of earlier methods of printing and bookmaking, of compositors' and proofreaders' habits, and of all the conditions under which a manuscript text was transferred to type. Examination of a printed text by a scholar with sufficient knowledge of these matters, if done in minute detail and with infinite pains, can tell a surprising amount—it can, for example, show that at given points in the setting up of the text a new compositor took over (with his own habits), it can demonstrate the order in which parts of a book were set up, it can by an examination of variants within a single issue show how certain corrections were made in the course of printing and infer the nature and meaning of these corrections. Endless patience in examining the physical aspects of a book is thus one prime requisite of the modern textual critic. Recent American textual critics have shown such patience together with an ingenuity and a thoroughness that make the great pioneer English bibliographers look like amateurs in comparison.

An example of the kind of resourcefulness brought to bear on textual studies by American scholarship is C. J. K. Hinman's collating machine. There are some 230 extant copies of the First Folio of Shakespeare, and the textual variations among these are significant. It would be an endless labor to collate even a part of this number of copies, but by inventing a machine that throws on a screen alternate images of the same page in two differnt copies Hinman has been able to reveal the most minute differences in the types at about fifty times the speed of ordinary collation. Hinman's first report of his work with the machine was made in 1947 ("Mechanized Collation: A Preliminary Report," *Papers of the Bibliographical Society of America,* XLI, 1947). Hinman's ultimate objective is to provide an exact account of how each page of each play of the Folio was put into type, identifying the compositor and the order of printing in each case. This in turn will put the problem of relating the printed text to the manuscript copy on a wholly new footing. Hinman's identification of "Compositor E," an apprentice whose work was full of mistakes and had to be corrected (in the various extant copies of the Folio there are examples of his work in both the corrected and the uncorrected state) is a brilliant piece of bibliographical detective work that throws a flood of light on textual problems of the Folio. (C. K. Hinman, "The Prentice Hand in the Tragedies of the Shakespeare First Folio: Compositor E," *Studies in Bibliography,* IX, 1956.)

The periodical just cited, in which Hinman's article on Compositor E appeared, was founded in 1948 as *Papers of the Bibliographical Society of the University of Virginia* by Fredson Bowers, one of the most brilliant and influential of contemporary bibliographers and textual critics. His edition of the plays of Thomas Dekker (4 vols., 1953-61) is the contemporary equivalent of what McKerrow's edition of Nashe was in its day—an edition that uses with enormous skill and patience all the resources provided by the most recent bibliographical knowledge and techniques. Bowers' work has been quite varied, ranging from such detailed studies as an investigation of variations in line-lengths as a clue to identifying the typesetting of different compositors ("Bibliographical Evidence From the Printer's Measure," *Studies in Bibliography,* II, 1949) and identifying one of the printers of the Fourth Folio from the ornamental initials he used ("Robert Roberts: A Printer of Shakespeare's Fourth Folio," *Shakespeare Quarterly,* II, 1951) to his edition of Dekker and his two brilliant justifications of his kind of bibliographical and textual studies—*Textual and Literary Criticism* (1959) and *The Bibliographical Way* (1959).

Among Bowers' many important and influential essays may be mentioned "Bibliography, Pure Bibliography, and Literary Studies" (*Papers of the Bibliographical Society of America,* XLVI, 1952) and "A Definitive Text of Shakespeare: Problems and Methods" (*Studies in Shakespeare,* 1953). In the latter of these Bowers shows himself alive to the anxiety of some scholars and critics that the elaboration of complex and specialized bibliographical techniques "may so widen the division between the bibliographer and the student of literature that it will be impossible even for the textual critic to use without difficulty some of the technical devices now employed in the analysis of the physical makeup of a book" as well as to the fears of those who anticipate "a conception of pure bibliography, written by bibliographers for bibliographers." He reassures his readers by distinguishing and defining five different kinds of bibliography and showing the significance and relevance of each. One of the most interesting aspects of Bowers' work—and this cannot be said of all American bibliographers—is his sensitivity to the charge of meaningless ultraspecialization and his concern with defending and explaining the meaning of his research and its value for literary study.

I have dwelt at some length on the work of Bowers and on the American trend that it represents because this trend has caused some concern outside America—there are English critics who wash their hands entirely of what they consider to be extravagantly "scientific" (in a pejorative sense) techniques for establishing a text. The defense of this kind of work ultimately is that before the literary critic can confidently analyze and evaluate a literary work he must be sure that he has before him what his author really wrote and not something marred, perhaps at some crucial point, by misprints and proofreaders' guesses, or simply an untrustworthy copy-text. There are many American scholars whose work I might have mentioned who have contributed to this kind of investigation of Shakespeare as of other writers, but a survey such as this one must be content with singling out a few examples. A good cross section of the kind of work being done is shown in the bibliographical papers read before the English Institute in 1949; these were subsequently published in the Virginia *Studies in Bibliography* and include "Editorial Problems—a Preliminary Survey" by R. C. Bald, "The Rationale of Copy-Text" by W. W. Greg (a contribution sent from England by this veteran bibliographer and read for him in his absence), "Some Relations of Bibliography to Editorial Problems" by Fredson Bowers, and "Some Postulates for Distributional Study of Texts" by Archibald A. Hill.

In general, the modern American achievement in Shakespearean scholarship and criticism is impressive. I have not, it is true, tried to work out the proportion of illuminating and helpful work to the work of the fools and the freaks, and it may well be true that, with such a large number of people engaged in writing about Shakespeare, there is more nonsense than sense produced. My concern has been with the sense— and, whatever proportion to the whole it may be, it is certainly a very considerable amount. In making Shakespeare available and understandable to the ordinary student; in interpreting his mind, his art, his stage, and his work in relation to his times; in illuminating the transmission of his text and clarifying the job of an editor—in all these matters modern American scholarship has a noble record. To emerge from an extended stay among these works is to emerge exhausted, it is true, but thoroughly impressed and genuinely enlightened. I am not sure that such a generalization would be wholly true of the modern American work in any other area of English studies.

4

A VARIETY OF INTERESTS
AND APPROACHES

The number of American literary scholars and critics who concentrate on medieval studies is smaller than it used to be; the decline of the old philological tradition has made this inevitable. Nevertheless, a substantial amount of work on Old and Middle English literature has been done in America in recent years, and it is perhaps surprising to find that it is an American who has written the one modern book-length study of Old English literature, *The Literature of the Anglo-Saxons* by George K. Anderson (1949). This, together with the same author's contribution to the composite *History of English Literature,* edited by Hardin Craig (1950) and Kemp Malone's and A. C. Baugh's share of *A Literary History of England,* edited by Baugh (1948), suggest that American medievalists in the field of English literature have not been spending all their time in minute philological investigation. ("Old English *swa* in Worn-down Correlative Clauses" is one of my favorite titles of the latter kind.) Indeed, the obvious necessity of providing historical background for an understanding of early works has kept the medieval field in large measure outside the war between critics and literary historians and has kept philology, history, and criticism working together in medieval studies to a greater extent than is common elsewhere.

Naturally enough, medieval studies concentrate on Chaucer, and if no one in recent years has emulated the heroic endeavors of J. M. Manly and Edith Rickert and if the mingling of scholarship and a common-sense humane criticism in the work of such older writers on Chaucer as G. L. Kittredge, R. K. Root, J. P. S. Tatlock, and John Livingston Lowes now represents a bygone mode, nevertheless the American tradition of Chaucer scholarship has been nobly kept up. One might note a slight problem of dates in comparing the older American Chaucerians with the more recent. Manly and Rickert's monumental eight-volume edition of *The Text of the Canterbury Tales* appeared as late as 1940, after the death of both editors, and even F. N. Robinson—the second, revised edition of whose invaluable one-volume edition of Chaucer's *Complete Works* appeared as recently as 1957—belonged to an older generation. Tatlock's *The Mind and Art of Chaucer* appeared posthumously in 1950. G. K. Anderson has noted that the ratio of books and articles on Chaucer produced in America to those produced in England has continued for some time to run at about three to one. Whatever the reasons, Americans have for long had a special interest in Chaucer.

Chaucer is represented in many World Literature courses, either by one of the *Canterbury Tales* or by *Troilus and Criseyde,* and is found by most American students to be the most directly accessible of medieval writers. A considerable amount of work, both historical and interpretative, has been done on the *Troilus* (e.g., Thomas A. Kirby's *Chaucer's Troilus: A Study in Courtly Love,* 1940) and occasionally a non-Chaucerian, having become interested in the poem while teaching it in a Great Books course, has published a critical article on some aspect of its structure or of the characterization in relation to the action. There are two modern translations, one in prose by R. M. Lumiansky (1951), who has also produced a prose translation of the *Canterbury Tales* (1948).

There have been several modern verse translations of the *Canterbury Tales*. So long as students are expected to read Chaucer without being given any instruction at all in Middle English, translations are bound to be produced and read; yet so much is missed in reading Chaucer in a modern rendering, and the effort required to master his language is so relatively small, that one cannot help regretting the vogue for Chaucer in translation. The fact is that students are often put off by the unfamiliar look of Chaucer's English; seventeenth and eighteenth century texts, which look more modern, are often almost as difficult for modern students with no training in the history of the language, but they do not realize this and read with cheerful misunderstanding.

The bulk of the scholarly and critical work done on Chaucer has been, as might be expected, on the *Canterbury Tales*. This has not significantly changed direction in the last thirty years. It ranged from minute textual or paleographical inquiries ("A Chaucer Scribe's Concern with Page Format," by T. A. Stroud, *Speculum,* **XXIII**, 1948) to such a comprehensive critical-cum-historical-cum-biographical study as W. W. Lawrence's *Chaucer and the Canterbury Tales* (1950). Manly's investigation of possible originals for the Canterbury pilgrims has been developed by several scholars. The intended order of the tales—which involves consideration of Chaucer's whole design for the work—has come in for careful investigation, and the many articles on this question by Germaine Dempster have been outstanding. There have been many interpretations and reinterpretations of *The Knight's Tale,* long a favorite of the critics, and the sources of a number of the tales have been carefully inquired into. There is the usual quota of dull or irrelevant fact hunting and speculation.

The Arthurian stories have a perpetual fascination for the student of medieval literature, and the American contribution here has been notable. The numerous articles by R. S. Loomis, which include his studies of the origins of the Grail legend, show historical literary scholarship at its most responsible and illuminating. Loomis has also edited an important collection of essays on the Arthurian romances, *Arthurian Literature in the Middle Ages: A Collaborative History* (1959). Any investigation of the Arthurian material is bound to be in some degree historical and genetic—concerned with origins, developments, influences, transfigurations, interrelationships—requiring linguistic, historical, and anthropological skills, among others. Mere critical exhibitionism cannot get very far in this kind of study, which has as a rule attracted only the most versatile scholars. *Arthurian Legends in Medieval Art* (1938) by R. S. and L. H. Loomis shows the literary scholar carrying his investigation into the visual arts to produce an important study of real originality. A. C. L. Brown's *The Origin of the Grail Legend* (1943) is an important study of a thorny subject. J. S. P. Tatlock's *The Legendary History of Britain: Geoffrey of Monmouth's Historia Regum Britanniae and Its Early Vernacular Versions* is a fine work of scholarship that authoritatively clarifies a complex and difficult subject.

Another great challenge to critics and scholars, as well as one of the best of all Middle English romances, is *Sir Gawain*

and the Green Knight, on which Kittredge wrote an important book in 1916. This fascinating and difficult work ap-
peals equally to the linguist, the metrist, the anthropologist,
the folklorist, the student of Arthurian romance, and the
New Critic. However, it does not appear to have been taken
up as a medieval classic to be read in colleges along with
Chaucer in the way that it has in many English universities,
and modern American writing on the subject reflects this
relative lack of general literary interest, for it is on the whole
scrappy and concerned with isolated details. Scholars have
discussed the meaning of certain words and phrases, debated
whether the poem is a vegetation myth, inquired into the
identity of the hero and of the author, discussed the color
symbolism, made observations on the structure, examined the
versification, and speculated on the "meaning." *The Gawain-
Poet: Studies in his Personality and Background* (1956) by
H. L. Savage is the only recent book-length treatment of
some of the problems connected with the poem and its authorship, and its concern is not primarily with the poem as
a poem. The New Critics, who in England keep returning to
the poem with fascination, do not seem to have had the cour-
age to tackle it in America (it is linguistically very difficult).

As usual, American scholars can be counted on to supply
the bibliographies. There are J. E. Wells's *A Manual of the
Writings in Middle English, 1050-1400* (1916, with nine
supplements, 1919-52), Loomis's *Introduction to Medieval
Literature, Chiefly in England* (1938, 1948), and many bibliographies of particular topics. R. S. Loomis and Rudolph
Willard have produced a volume of *Medieval English Verse
and Prose in Modernized Versions* (1948), and several college anthologies of English literature contain translations of

73

both Anglo-Saxon and Middle English works, together with
both Anglo-Saxon and Middle English works, together with
The College Survey of English Literature (1949) edited by
B. J. Whiting, F. B. Millett, *et al.* includes among other
Anglo-Saxon and Middle English items, prose translations of
Beowulf, The Dream of the Rood, and *Sir Gawain and the
Green Knight* as well as extracts from *Piers Plowman* and
the *Canterbury Tales* in the original, with the words glossed
at the foot of the page. Tools for the scholar and representa-
tive texts (of a kind) for the nonspecialist student—these are
the two extremes between which much modern American
medieval literary scholarship moves. This is roughly true of
American literary scholarship in other fields also. It is in the
middle ground between these extremes—the provision of
large interpretative critical and scholarly works not addressed
exclusively to other experts but meant also for the intelligent general reader (such as *The Allegory of Love* by the
English scholar and critic C. S. Lewis) that American per-
formance is relatively barren. Does this mean that the "general reader" of serious critical and scholarly books hardly
exists in America?

The interest in medieval drama found in many of the older
generation of American scholars has noticeably declined in
recent years. Karl Young's comprehensive study, *The Drama
of the Medieval Church* (2 vols., 1933) and Hardin Craig's
English Religious Drama of the Middle Ages (1955)—
historicodescriptive in method—are two of the most impressive works on this topic, but younger scholars have not much
cultivated the field. Sixteenth and seventeenth century drama
continues, naturally enough, to claim most attention.

That there should have been in the last thirty years or so a

74

spate of activity on the seventeenth century (apart from Milton) is not surprising in view of the use made of the seventeenth century, particularly of Donne and the metaphysicals, in the modern revolution in poetic taste. Articles, explications, and critical footnotes of all kinds dealing with Donne or with other of the metaphysical poets have flowed in a steady stream since the early 1930's, though there has been a slackening off in the last year or two. Some of these articles are mere pieces of barren ingenuity, others are perceptive and illuminating. Many critical studies of modern poetry—notably Cleanth Brooks's *Modern Poetry and the Tradition* (1939) and William Van O'Connor's *Sense and Sensibility in Modern Poetry* (1948)—begin with Donne and the seventeenth century poets in order to illustrate the proper use of metaphor. "The significant relationship between the modernist poets and the seventeenth-century poets of wit lies here—in their common conception of the use of metaphor," wrote Brooks. "The significant relationship is indicated by the fact that the metaphysical poets and the modernists stand opposed to both the neoclassic and Romantic poets on the issue of metaphor." Eliot's famous remark that "in the seventeenth century a dissociation of sensibility set in, from which we have never recovered" is accepted by O'Connor and others as the clue to the importance of the seventeenth century poets in restoring the true tradition of English poetry; both Brooks's and O'Connor's books are in fact accounts of the nature of that tradition and its restoration by certain modern poets, notably Yeats and Eliot. The positively scriptural use of Eliot's essay on the metaphysical poets (as well as of other of his essays and remarks) becomes extremely tedious by the time we get to the 1940's, and it is refreshing to find some recent critics challenging Eliot's whole position on dissociated sensibility.

The history of English poetry was rewritten (in outline, at least) in the light of Eliot's analysis of what happened to the English poetic mind in the late seventeenth century. Donne replaced Milton or Spenser as the great poet of the English Renaissance, and Hopkins replaced Tennyson as the great Victorian poet. It is interesting to see how, having thrown out much of English poetry between Donne and Hopkins and constructed a metaphysical-cum-symbolist definition of poetry to justify the procedure, the New Critics have one by one been letting in the excluded poets by the back door. Pope was soon admitted (perhaps in some degree under the influence of the English critic F. R. Leavis's persuasive contention that he was in the true "line of wit"); Gray's "Elegy" was shown to be ironic and ambivalent; the best of Wordsworth's poetry was similarly analyzed as though it were Donne's and found to respond to the treatment; and Tennyson himself was welcomed back into the fold with labored analyses of his simpler lyric poems. Of the romantic poets, Keats was first restored, for the richness of his odes allows of any degree of subtlety in interpretation, and Byron's irony gave him an obvious entrée. Only Shelley remains exiled, as "Platonic" (in Ransom's sense), or infantile, or lacking in irony, or naïvely utopian—for original sin comes into this revaluation, originally from T. E. Hulme. Great poetry, it is argued, cannot be written without a belief in "the radical imperfectibility of man"—which, it is alleged, Shelley was too naïve to share—and it is the rediscovery of that belief, says O'Connor, echoing earlier modern critics, that is producing a fruitful "new vision of the world."

76

What is involved here is a change in modern poetic taste, closely related to a change in the placing of the seventeenth century poets. (What is involved is also a change in fashion; scores of articles on this topic over the last thirty years are fashionable and nothing more.) The scholar and the avant-garde critic therefore come together more often in work on seventeenth century poetry than in any other area of English literature. George Williamson's *The Donne Tradition* (1930) was one of the first books on the poet to look at him from this larger perspective (Williamson has also written on Eliot). *A Garland for John Donne* (1932) by Theodore Spencer and others is a collection of essays that similarly extended the significance of the study of Donne. Milton A. Rugoff's *Donne's Imagery: A Study in Creative Sources* (1939) and Leonard Unger's *Donne's Poetry and Modern Criticism* (1950) sum up with great skill and knowledge different aspects of the Donne cult.

Of the other metaphysical poets, Marvell has provoked the greatest number of explicatory essays after Donne, while Herbert has been taken out of the hands of libertine modern critics and restored to his own contemporary tradition by Rosamund Tuve's work of formidable scholarship, *A Reading of George Herbert.* Joseph H. Summers' *George Herbert* (1954) is a distinguished modern study of the poet, his thought and his poetic techniques, which combines the methods of modern critical analysis with a thorough knowledge of the traditions within which Herbert worked.

Modern American scholarship on and criticism of Pope combines—in a rather different way from the combination of scholarship and New Criticism on Donne—historical, textual, and biographical scholarship with new critical subtlety.

77

As an example of this, the work of Maynard Mack may be singled out. The other early eighteenth century writer who has attracted the attention of some of America's best scholars and critics is Jonathan Swift, whose reputation has never stood higher. The two books by Richard Quintana, *The Mind and Art of Jonathan Swift* (1936) and *Swift: An Introduction* (1955) are comprehensive biocritical studies in an older tradition but none the less useful for that. Important ground has been broken on the biographical side by Louis Landa in his *Swift and the Church of Ireland* (1954), but perhaps the most interesting as well as the most characteristic recent American work on Swift has been studies of his satirical techniques, his varieties of irony, and his rhetorical devices. J. M. Bullitt's *Jonathan Swift and the Anatomy of Satire* (1953), Martin Price's *Swift's Rhetorical Art* (1953), and W. B. Ewald's *The Masks of Jonathan Swift* (1954) are intelligent and sophisticated studies of Swift's ways of putting his intentions into art. Interest in rhetorical techniques has, incidentally, been growing in America in recent years. A Ph.D. dissertation at Vanderbilt University in 1939 had the title "The Function of Classical Rhetoric in Swift's Major Ironical Essays"—a subject that some years ago would have been considered highly pedantic but that now represents an approach respected by scholars and critics alike.

This study, it must again be emphasized, is not a catalog of work done period by period, even of the most important work done on the most important writers; individual items are picked out only to illustrate trends and methods. I shall say nothing, therefore, of the mass of American work done on other eighteenth century writers, but will pause only to note that the high esteem now enjoyed by Dr. Johnson shows how premature was Cleanth Brooks's lumping in 1939 of "neoclassics and Romantics" as opposed to modernists. (Not that Johnson was strictly a neoclassic, but that is to pursue a quite different question.) It is perhaps paradoxical that some of the most subtle critical minds in modern America have been concerned to provide appreciative analyses of Johnson's critical method, in spite of the fact that Johnson condemned the metaphysical style, or at least damned it with faint praise. Quite apart from the Yale "Boswell factory," and quite apart from the fine scholarly work on Johnson done by James L. Clifford, E. L. McAdam, and others, and apart too from those two excellent (but very different) general studies of Johnson, Joseph Wood Krutch's *Samuel Johnson* (1944) and Walter Jackson Bate's *The Achievement of Samuel Johnson* (1955), we find on the one hand the meticulously detailed, highly sophisticated study of *The Prose Style of Samuel Johnson* (1941) by W. K. Wimsatt and on the other the finely reasoned exposition of Johnson's critical principles by W. R. Keast, "The Theoretical Foundations of Johnson's Criticism" (in *Critics and Criticism,* edited by R. S. Crane, 1952). Keast's article on "Johnson's Criticism of the Metaphysical Poets" (*ELH,* XVII, 1950) is another definitive essay on an important aspect of Johnson's criticism, more lucid and more relevant than Allen Tate's oddly congested essay on the same subject, "Johnson on the Metaphysicals" (*Kenyon Review,* XI, 1949). (Keast was trained by Crane at Chicago. Crane's own methodological skill in discussing the criticism of others is brilliantly shown in his small masterpiece of exposition, "English Neoclassical Criticism: An Outline Sketch," first written for *The Dictionary of World Literature,* edited by Joseph T. Shipley, 1943, and reprinted in *Critics and Criticism.*)

The place of the romantic poets in American literary study has been much influenced by the two great antiromantic waves that have hit American criticism in the present century. The first is that of Irving Babbitt and the New Humanists. Though this movement flourished before the period with which I am dealing, its direct and (more especially) indirect influence on recent critical attitudes has been considerable. For the New Humanism was much more than an antiromantic movement in criticism; it also represented a general attack on the Harvard philological tradition of literary study and teaching of a kind that foreshadowed the later conflict between historical and "pure" literary critics. Babbitt and the other originator of the movement, Paul Elmer More, were the only two students in Professor Charles R. Lanman's Sanskrit class at Harvard in 1892-93; Lanman was also T. S. Eliot's teacher, and it is significant that Lanman's article on "Hindu Law and Custom as to Gifts" in the *Kittredge Anniversary Papers* of 1913 contains all the Sanskrit material (including the fable of the thunder and the stress on the moral importance of "giving" in Hindu thought) that Eliot was to use in *The Waste Land* (though in his notes Eliot prefers to cite Deussen's *Sechzig Upanishads des Veda*). This calling in of the Far East to redress the balance of the West was an important part of the new movement, which has had interesting consequences in some rather unexpected fields. (One wonders if there is a direct line between the study of Indic philosophy that the avant-garde went in for at Harvard in the first decade of this century and the present popularity of Zen Buddhism.)

In Babbitt's thought this was but one element in a program that called for order, control, classical balance, and restraint in literature and that held up classical French literature as the model. Babbitt taught French at Harvard, though he did not get his professorship until 1912, much to the indignation of More, who in a letter to Stuart P. Sherman had called it an "outrageous scandal" that Babbitt had not yet been promoted. More resigned from the academic profession after a few years of teaching and retired to Shelburne, New Hampshire, to become eventually literary editor and then editor-in-chief of the *Nation*. He spent the last twenty-two years of his life (1915-37) in retirement at Princeton, where he was a potent influence. This refusal to stay in the regular academic profession was More's protest against the Ph.D. system and the whole German-inspired tradition of scholarship and teaching that had been developed in order to show that literature was not a subject for the dilettante. Just as later critics have urged that criticism has its own strenuous discipline and does not need to depend on a stiffening of philology to keep away the mere dabblers, so the New Humanists held that the discovery and skilled advocacy of the proper kind of moral order in works of literary art were both a difficult and a necessary task for the literary student and that scholars like Kittredge had reduced the study of literature to (in More's phrase) a "killing pedantry."

Babbitt was the great propagandist of the movement, of which he remained the center, though More did his share from his extra-academic editorial position. More came increasingly to believe that a nonreligious humanism was inadequate; on this point he was with Eliot and against Babbitt. Thus the Hulme-Eliot line, so potent in modern criticism and so influential in defining the terms of modern antiromanticism, can also be seen as a Babbitt-More-Eliot line, and the significance of the New Humanism, both as the first important revolt against the Kittredge tradition in literary study and as the first modern formulation of a critical position both antiromantic and antiphilological, becomes evident. The excitement about the New Humanism took a considerable time to spread beyond Harvard and Princeton; it boiled up on a national scale in the late 1920's. The doctrine was spread in the Midwest by Norman Foerster (who had been a contemporary of Eliot's at Harvard), who in 1930 went to the University of Iowa as director of the School of Letters in an attempt to rescue literary study from the philologists and source-hunters. But by this time other currents were making themselves felt and the direct influence of the New Humanism steadily declined.

These other currents included the second antiromantic movement of the Hulme-Eliot tradition, though this, as we have seen, had its relation, through the Eliot-More connection, with the first. This movement was much more widespread and in the 1930's rapidly became the fashionable critical creed of the younger literary critics at the universities. It was stimulated by such influential essays as Leavis's on Shelley (1935) and Robert Penn Warren's witty and widely read "Pure and Impure Poetry" (1943) which contains a mocking analysis of a lyric by Shelley that is very difficult to resist. Leavis wrote:

That "quivering intensity," offered in itself apart from any substance, offered instead of any object, is what, though it may make Shelley intoxicating at fifteen, makes him almost unreadable, except in very small quantities of his best, to the mature . . . ; the elusive imagery, the high-pitched emotions, the tone and movement, the ardours, ecstasies and despairs, are too much the same all through.

Both of these essays are included in a much-used anthology of New Critical texts, a book that sums up what American literary students have been reading and believing for a generation, *Critiques and Essays in Criticism 1920-1948* (1949), edited by Robert W. Stallman.

The result has been a host of critical articles on similar lines, many of them merely exercises in a current fashion. Every tyro can now explain why "Trees" is a bad poem (which it is; though with less effort than some recent critics have expended on proving Tennyson paradoxical it could be "proved" to be full of paradoxes and ambiguities) and at the same time the typical young American academic critic of the last twenty-five years is acutely embarrassed by such a simple lyrical utterance as, say, Burns's "A Red, Red Rose" and just does not know what to do with it. Nevertheless, while it is inevitable that with literary study conducted on such an enormous scale as it is in modern America there should be a great deal of fashionable critical writing of little or no permanent value, there have been some important attacks from the other side.

There is a small but flourishing band of scholars and critics who set their faces against the dominant modern tradition and devote themselves to a rehabilitation of the more vulnerable romantic poets. Blake is easily recoverable because of his great mythmaking capacities and his use of symbol, and because myth and symbol are major interests of the modern critic. Blake the myth maker and mask wearer (the Blake that is nearest Yeats, in fact) is the concern of Mark Schorer in his *William Blake: The Politics of Vision* (1946), and there have been many cunning explications of particular Blake lyrics. There have also been some interesting attempts to show that the romantic poets were responsibly and admirably involved in the politics of their day. Thus David V. Erdman's *Blake, Prophet Against Empire: A Poet's Interpretation of the History of his own Times* (1954) sees Blake in relation to the social and political problems of his day, more in the manner of the English Jacob Bronowski, in his *William Blake, 1757-1827: A Man Without a Mask* (1944), than in that of Milton O. Percival, whose *William Blake's Circle of Destiny* (1938) discusses Blake's use of old esoteric traditions. Jungian critics, and those interested in mythological archetypes, have examined and often vindicated Blake's Prophetic Books. The most sustained and sympathetic presentation of Blake as myth maker is by the Canadian critic Northrop Frye (*Fearful Symmetry*, 1947), whose work has had great influence on American Blake studies as well as in encouraging a more general revival of appreciation of romantic poetry (as in the work of Harold Bloom at Yale). There have been several studies that take Blake and Yeats together, and merely to set Blake in such company is, in the eyes of the modern critic, to vindicate him thoroughly.

Attempts to show that such poets as Blake and Shelley were not muling visionaries but responsible poets have been made both by a demonstration of the logic and coherence of their imagery and symbolism and by showing their serious concern with the thought and problems of their day. K. N. Cameron's *The Young Shelley* (1950) examines the development of Shelley's radicalism and shows it to be well thought out and far from vacuously utopian, while the preoccupation of Joseph Barrell's *Shelley and the Thought of his Time* (1947) is indicated by its title. Indeed, the rehabilitation of Shelley as a thinker has been one of the main tasks of American Shelley scholarship ever since Carl Grabo's publications of the 1930's, of which the most important is *The Magic Plant: The Growth of Shelley's Thought* (1936). Richard H. Fogle defended Shelley against the New Critics in his "Romantic Bards and Metaphysical Reviewers" (*ELH,* XII, 1945) and Carlos Baker, in his *Shelley's Major Poetry: The Fabric of a Vision* (1948), as well as Fogle, in his *The Imagery of Keats and Shelley* (1949), gave generous and sympathetic consideration to Shelley's poetry as unquestionably "major." In short, while Shelley has borne the brunt of the antiromantic critical attack, defenders of both his intellectual responsibility and his poetic effectiveness have not been lacking. Whatever one's views of Shelley, one cannot but welcome this failure of critical *Gleichschaltung.*

Before leaving Blake and Shelley, I should note that the attack on them was on two quite different grounds, one (springing originally from the New Humanism as well as from Hulme and Eliot) that they had no external tradition of order and intellectual and moral discipline but were eccentric and undisciplined individualists, and the other that they lacked the wit and complexity of the greatest poets. The defenders of Shelley have concerned themselves with both these lines of argument and their counterattack has therefore been on two fronts.

Quite apart from the attack on and defense of certain romantic poets was the controversy—an interesting by-product of the quarrel between history and criticism—over whether such a phenomenon as romanticism can usefully be discussed as a whole, and indeed whether the romantic movement ever existed. The symposium on romanticism in the *Journal of the History of Ideas* (II, 1941) and René Wellek's "The Concept of Romanticism in Literary History" (arguing that the term can profitably be used) are among the documents produced by this argument.

The impressive American work in the production of biographies and the editing of the letters of Victorian writers is discussed in a later section, but modern American interest in the Victorian extends far beyond this kind of scholarship. There is an interest in their problems, a concern with their dilemmas, and a deep curiosity about their ways of thinking and feeling. Richard D. Altick's study of *The English Common Reader . . . 1800-1900* (1957) investigates the development and the nature of mass reading in the nineteenth century as a contribution to an awareness of the problems of our own culture; this sense of the relevance of the Victorians is commonly found and it gives much of the work done on them a special kind of excitement. The interest in Matthew Arnold, which has produced among much else Lionel Trilling's notable *Matthew Arnold* (1939) and E. K. Brown's *Matthew Arnold: A Study in Conflict* (1948), derives in large measure from a sense of the contemporariness of his intellectual and moral situation. The attention paid by literary scholars to Darwin and to the impact of *The Origin of Species* on the Victorians is of a similar kind. One of the most interesting works produced by this sort of attention is the volume edited by Philip Appleman, William Madden, and Michael Wolff to mark the hundredth anniversary of the publication of *The Origin of Species—1859: Entering an Age of Crisis* (1959), with its division into three sections, "Science, Religion and the Critical Mind," "Patterns of National Development," and "The Challenge of Popular Culture." J. H. Buckley's *The Victorian Temper: A Study in Literary Culture* (1952) and the eleven essays in *The Reinterpretation of Victorian Literature* (1950), edited by J. E. Baker, also, in different ways, give evidence of a sense of the contemporary relevance of the Victorians. There are of course the usual handbooks, study-aids, and anthologies for this period as for others—characteristic American contributions—and critical essays on individual Victorian novels, both as prefaces to college editions and in periodicals.

Much modern American criticism of fiction takes its cue from James, and in doing so has developed its own tools for the investigation of "point of view" as a central aspect of the novel-writer's art. (Norman Friedman's "Point of View in Fiction: The Development of a Critical Concept," *PMLA,* 1955, gives an account of this important movement in criticism.) An influential essay in this tradition, much used in criticism classes, is Mark Schorer's "Technique as Discovery" (*Hudson Review,* 1948). Together with this there has been a rapid growth of interest in symbolic patterns and in structural and thematic movement, and the old fashioned discussion of fiction in terms of separable plot, characters, and setting is generally scorned. The new method, or methods, has

87

its dangers, as a look at some recent articles in *Nineteenth Century Fiction* will show—an insistence on finding ironic counterstatements whether they are really there or not, or forcing patterns of symbolic suggestion, or employing kinds of sophistication inappropriate to the art involved (as Marvin Mudrick does in his sometimes brilliant and sometimes perverse *Jane Austen: Irony as Defense and Discovery,* 1952). On the whole, however, the application of these new critical tools has brought a welcome liveliness to the discussion of Victorian as of modern fiction; some of the recent work on Dickens, George Eliot, the Brontës, Hardy, James, and Conrad, and on the modern short story, has been thoroughly impressive. At the same time there has been a lot of nonsense talked, probably more about *Wuthering Heights* than any other nineteenth century novel. Besides James, and those critics who stem from him, such as Percy Lubbock, one should note Leavis's *The Great Tradition* (1948) as a potent influence on modern American criticism of Victorian fiction. Out of the numerous scholarly discussions of aspects of Victorian writers, one might single out Fanny Ratchford's *The Brontës' Web of Childhood* (1941), which investigates the young Brontës' childhood stories and their significance for an understanding of how their imagination worked.

Work on the Victorian poets has on the whole been less interesting than that on the novelists. The general books on the Victorians contain some interesting investigations of the dilemmas and double voices of Tennyson and others, and there have been more extended attempts to show that Tennyson and Browning as well as Arnold were divided and "alienated" (e.g., E. D. H. Johnson's *The Alien Vision of Victorian Poetry,* 1952) and therefore acceptable to the modern reader. Paull F. Baum, in his *Tennyson Sixty Years After* (1948), presented a judicious weighing of the poet's qualities and limitations, and on the whole a note of moderate approval is now the one most commonly found in discussions of Tennyson and Browning. Arnold, an honorary twentieth century writer, is in a class by himself. Browning, so long the subject of overintent explanatory studies, has largely won free of that kind of treatment, with generally beneficial results to his reputation, although his influence on Pound and Eliot has never been adequately recognized.

Reference is made elsewhere to the tendency in some quarters to treat a lyric of Tennyson as though it were a metaphysical poem. *Critical Essays on the Poetry of Tennyson,* edited by John Killham (1960), contains essays by critics on both sides of the Atlantic and gives a fair picture of the present reputation of that most Victorian of Victorian poets. It includes T. S. Eliot's 1936 essay, "In Memoriam," with its equivocal opening: "Tennyson is a great poet, for reasons that are perfectly clear." This essay certainly played its part in keeping Tennyson alive as an object of serious critical attention in an age when the whole poetic and critical fashion was set firmly against him.

With some exceptions that have been noted, modern American work on the Victorians has been remarkably independent and free from the compulsion to adjust to prevailing winds of fashion. One has the feeling that there are more scholars and critics of the Victorian period than of other periods who are in the field because they are interested, and also that (witness the founding in 1957 of *Victorian Studies*) they have an interest in the period as a whole that transcends the quarrel between historians and critics.

89

5

LITERARY CRITICISM AND
LITERARY HISTORY

When, as a young man in my middle twenties, I was invited
by President Hutchins to leave Oxford in order to come and
teach at the University of Chicago, my knowledge of the
American achievement in English studies was, I suppose,
typical of that of most graduates in English literature of a
British university. F. N. Robinson's invaluable one-volume
edition of Chaucer had appeared in 1933, when I was in my
third year at Edinburgh University, and I had acquired it
almost at once, as it was clear from the reviews that it collected in one volume almost everything that a university
student of Chaucer ought to know. I knew also the important
edition of selected *Canterbury Tales* by J. M. Manly (1928)
and Manly and Edith Rickert had been pointed out to me in
the Bodleian Library, Oxford, as they worked there on what
was to be their great eight-volume edition of *The Text of the
Canterbury Tales* (1940). I also knew the books on Chaucer
by R. K. Root (*The Poetry of Chaucer,* 1906), G. L. Kittredge (*Chaucer and His Poetry,* 1915), Manly (*Some New
Light on Chaucer,* 1926), and John Livingston Lowes (*Geoffrey Chaucer,* 1934—lectures delivered on the William J.
Cooper Foundation at Swarthmore in 1932). I knew too,
and had found most valuable, Eleanor P. Hammond's anthology of *English Verse Between Chaucer and Surrey* (1927),
a collection that made available texts that were not easy to find

and that most students only read about in literary histories. I had used James H. Hanford's *A Milton Handbook* (1926), had read with fascination Lowes's study of the sources in Coleridge's reading of the images and ideas to be found in "The Ancient Mariner" and elsewhere (*The Road to Xanadu*, 1927), and I had read, partly in agreement and partly in irritation, two of Irving Babbitt's antiromantic critical studies, *Rousseau and Romanticism* (1919) and *On Being Creative and Other Essays* (1932). I had used J. E. Spingarn's *History of Literary Criticism in the Renaissance* (1899, 1925) as a short cut to a knowledge of Renaissance critical texts; in the library I had also browsed through his useful collection of *Critical Essays of the Seventeenth Century* (3 vols., 1908-09).

This composite picture of American literary scholarship as seen from Britain in the late 1930's was not wildly disproportionate. The older philological tradition of Kittredge's Harvard and Manly's Chicago was not yet extinct, though rapidly declining, and its monuments were known throughout the world. I am concerned in this essay only with the last thirty years or so, and it is therefore no part of my task to describe and evaluate the achievement of the older tradition, whose heyday was the early years of this century. But a word must be said about it, since it provided the background against which a variety of revolts—from Babbitt's New Humanism to Brooks and Warren's New Criticism—can alone be fully understood.

My old Edinburgh Professor, H. J. C. Grierson (later Sir Herbert Grierson), used to tell me that he kept compulsory Anglo-Saxon in the honors English curriculum at Aberdeen and Edinburgh as a "stiffening," to make sure that his students would get some real scholarly discipline and not indulge in mere impressionist gush. Now this notion that the academic study of a modern European literature must guard against mere belle-lettrism was common on both sides of the Atlantic at that stage in the development of humanities subjects when literature was fighting for recognition against such established subjects as classical philology, philosophy, and theology. The study of a literature written in one's own language was particularly suspect: would it not attract the superficial and the lazy, who would substitute critical chit-chat for real scholarship?

The modern answer is that literary criticism is a stringent intellectual discipline in its own right and is to be carried on by recognizing its precise differentiating qualities, not by adding bits of philological and historical difficulty to it in order to toughen it up. One scares away the lightweights by the complexity and the strenuousness of the means employed to describe, analyze, and evaluate a work of literary art, not by insisting that they learn Anglo-Saxon. This modern view is not so unambiguous as it may seem, and the results of applying it, as we shall see, have been various and sometimes unexpected. The older view was concerned to gain for the study of modern (i.e., postclassical) literature a respectability that it has now long since won. In serious academic literary work, holders of this view maintained, one should go far enough back in time so as to confront philological, historical, even paleographical difficulties, and in solving these and applying the knowledge brought by the solution to the reading of the given work a total view of its human significance could be achieved.

"The ideal philologist is at once antiquary, palaeographer,

grammarian, lexicologist, expounder, critic, historian of literature, and, above all, lover of humanity." These words were uttered by A. S. Cook in the course of his presidential address to the Modern Language Association in 1897, "The Province of English Philology," later printed in a volume of his essays, *The Higher Study of English* (1906). Cook was an Anglo-Saxonist, who edited many Anglo-Saxon texts, produced (with C. B. Tinker) two volumes of translations from Old English poetry and prose, edited *A Literary Middle English Reader* (1915) and Addison's essays on *Paradise Lost* (1892), and compiled a concordance to the English poems of Thomas Gray (1908). His work shows him combining most if not all of the skills he demanded of "the ideal philologist," or if not combining them at least using them seriatim. Whether the result is a fusion of the parts into a wholeness of insight into the human significance of given works of literary art demanded, ideally at least, by old and new critic alike, remains debatable.

As Cook saw it, his job was to find out what these works meant, by the use of appropriate historical and philological tools; that a proper understanding of their meaning as works of art required also some understanding of the special ways in which language works when employed in literary or poetic discourse as distinct from scientific or historical discourse would never have occurred to him any more than it would have occurred to Kittredge or Lowes. That is, they would all have conceded that of course language works differently in imaginative literature from the way it works in mere factual discourse but they would have treated this as a common-sense question rather than as a matter that involved subtle inquiry into such matters as ambivalence and tension. At least Cook

93

and his generation of literary scholars presented the texts, set them in their historical context, translated or explained the difficult words, and in short made it possible for students to learn to read them accurately. This generation of literary scholars excelled above all at putting older literary works in their historical contexts. Lowes's book on Chaucer is essentially an explanation of how the world of medieval ideas entered into Chaucer's writing that thus cannot be fully understood unless we learn something about the intellectual map of the world as it looked to a well-read layman of the fourteenth century.

When, then, I came to Chicago in September 1937 I was not prepared to meet there—as I did, violently and immediately—the view that the proper understanding and appreciation of literature had been corrupted by historical study and that the historically oriented "survey course" had been the archvillain of American academic education in literature. R. S. Crane, who had recently come under the influence of the new Aristotelianism of R. P. McKeon, had just produced a paper (which he showed me) entitled "The Two Modes of Criticism," in which he had distinguished Aristotelian or "meroscopic" criticism, which was concerned only with the unique structure of meanings within the given work of literary art, from Platonic or Coleridgean or "holoscopic" criticism, which regarded all knowledge as ultimately one and was free to include the whole universe (including the universe of ethical and political discourse) in its purview in discussing works of literature. The implication was clear that, whatever theoretical merits the Platonic mode possessed, the time was now ripe for a strong Aristotelian movement; indeed, some of the younger members of the "Chicago school" at that time used "Platonic" as a wholly pejorative term (though their use was not in the same sense as John Crowe Ransom's pejorative use of it) and reserved their admiration entirely for the "meroscopic" approach.

This is not the place to detail the development and ramifications of the Chicago school. Crane himself changed his mind on many important points as time went on and in recent years has come more and more to look for direct human implications in literature rather than to be content with brilliant demonstrations of complexities of structural pattern; other members of the original group have developed their own special methods and interests. (Crane's preface to the abridged edition of *Critics and Criticism,* 1957, shows some aspects of his later position; the volume itself, published in its unabridged form in 1952, is a good cross section of the Chicago school in its mature phase.)

The striking point about the Chicago group in the late 1930's is that they were agreed in putting literary criticism before literary history and in attacking literary history as an inevitably superficial as well as a distorting and vulgarizing way of teaching literature in universities. The function of the academic teacher of literature, they maintained, was to demonstrate the unique form of the individual literary work and to eschew generalizations that brought together in essentially meaningless unities groups of works under historical categories. Part of this protest against literary history arose from a sense of the inadequacy of the traditional survey course, which ploughed through literature chronologically, dishing out potted biographies of authors, summaries of plots, lists of adjectives applicable to particular styles and periods, and in general confused biography, history of ideas, literary description, and critical evaluation. It is true that the survey course always has a tendency to degenerate into some such medley, and it is true also that it enables a student to write with superficial confidence about works of literature that he has not read. Rigorous critical description and analysis at least demand careful reading and prevent students confusing generalizations *about* literature with the works of literature themselves. In his article, "History versus Criticism in the University Study of Literature" (*English Journal,* XXIV, 1935), Crane explained why criticism was to be preferred and what was to be gained by a proper use of criticism in the university classroom.

All this was in line with the general tendency of the New Criticism to insist on the differentiating qualities of the work of literary art and to develop rigorous techniques of analysis that eschewed biographical or "history of ideas" references. Not that the Chicago group was saying the same thing that John Crowe Ransom or Robert Penn Warren or Cleanth Brooks was saying—indeed, one of the sharpest and most closely reasoned attacks on Brooks's methods is to be found in Crane's essay, "Cleanth Brooks; or the Bankruptcy of Critical Monism" (*Modern Philology,* XLV, 1948), reprinted as "The Critical Monism of Cleanth Brooks" in *Critics and Criticism*—but the group was, in its early stages especially, one of the various elements in American academic life helping to oust the survey course in favor of the author course and to promote subtle analysis of the individual work at the expense of general discussion of authors or of periods.

The Chicago group derived their methods and ideas in large measure from their own interpretation of Aristotle's *Poetics* and other writing (it is important to note that they

96

did not confine themselves to the *Poetics* but were concerned with Aristotle's method in general) and were more philosophically professional and intellectually sophisticated than many of the New Critics, most of whom derived their ideas ultimately from T. E. Hulme, T. S. Eliot, I. A. Richards, F. R. Leavis, and William Empson in varying proportions and in varying degrees. Eliot had already been turned toward an antiromantic attitude by Irving Babbitt before he settled in England to come under the influence of Hulme's rather different kind of antiromanticism. The advocacy of the hard, dry, precise image, the attack on the view of literature as self-expression or as the expression of "personality," the insistence on the discipline of the craft rather than on the sublimity of the idea, the rehabilitation of stylization and its assocation with symbolism—all these elements came into the New Criticism from the Hulme-Eliot complex of ideas that found their way by a variety of routes back across the Atlantic in the 1920's and 1930's.

With this, as every schoolboy knows, came the depreciation of the Victorian elegiac mode in poetry and the exaltation of the seventeenth century metaphysical poets, of Gerard Manley Hopkins, of the sinewy idiom of certain Jacobean dramatists and the symbolist practices and ironic devices of certain late nineteenth century French poets. The members of the Chicago school never confined themselves to this new orthodoxy; they would tackle anything once they had found the appropriate "organon." Crane's article on "The Concept of Plot and the Plot of *Tom Jones*" (*Journal of General Education,* January 1950, reprinted with some alterations in *Critics and Criticism*) in both the object of its attention and in sheer intellectual adroitness went beyond any conventional

New Critical piece of analysis. Yet, if we view the critical scene as a whole, we can see the Chicago school as part of what might be called the new critical specialism, the revolution that dismissed reports of the reader's personal reactions to a work of art as "autobiography, not criticism"—this phrase was actually launched at an unfortunate student in Chicago in the late 1930's—and insisted that the lay reaction to a poem or a novel was irrelevant and that the job of the true student of literature was to cultivate ingenuities of analysis that seemed to have no immediate relationship to the reasons why great works of literature had been read, enjoyed, and valued by generations of readers.

The new movement attacked on two fronts. On the one hand it attacked historicism, relativism, and the loose confounding of life and letters; on the other it attacked impressionism, the assumption that a reader's report of his reactions on reading a given work constituted a valid piece of literary criticism. Part of the latter attack was in some degree bound up with the critic's desire to be as "scientific" as the scientists, to have as rigorous and as objective a method and indeed as specialized a vocabulary. The resulting paradox lay in the fact that it produced among vast numbers of students the very opposite of a scientific method, namely a straining after ingenuity for its own sake, a determination to read as many ambiguities and paradoxes into a particular work as could possibly be managed, a complete absence of any control in terms of which the total complex of meaning could be assessed and valued.

I can recollect from my own experience as Professor of English in America—and I am sure many of my American colleagues have had similar experiences—how often I vainly tried to persuade a clever but misguided student that there is an objective pattern of meaning in a work of literature that, however many valuable new implications one may discover, one cannot flout at will; that one cannot discuss a gay example of *vers de société* by Matthew Prior as though it were a poem by Donne or Hopkins; and that if one's ultimate analysis of the pattern of meaning totally reverses one's first impression of the kind of work it is, then something is radically wrong with the analysis. I was met with total skepticism: the whole process of practical criticism was regarded as a test of competitive ingenuity, a kind of game where the winner was the one who could force on the sense of the words the most paradoxes or the most ambiguities. This, it seems to me, has been a radical fault in much recent American academic criticism. If modern American criticism has shown sophistication, subtlety, intellectual power, unusual perceptiveness, brilliant responsiveness to the ways in which language can be used as a work of literary art—and it has at times shown all these qualities—it has also shown much barren cleverness, a dogged and (in the last resort) unintelligent ingenuity, a sense that the clever-clever analysis of a work is really more valuable than the work itself.

This is partly because the pressure to publish has impelled academics to produce more critical essays (as well as more academic written work of other kinds) than they are really interested in and on topics that they are not genuinely *inward* with. But there is another aspect of the problem, an aspect that has been seized on by those scholars who, having studied the modes and conventions available to a particular writer at a given time, reproach the critics for having taken no account of these factors and for irresponsibly interpreting works in a way that was thoroughly inconsistent with the world of ideas and conventions in which the writer lived and worked. Even on the purely linguistic level, it has been pointed out that language itself is a phenomenon that exists in time; the references and overtones of meaning that a word carries depend on when the word was used; and what might be seized upon by the critic as a strange or remarkable or unique usage might in fact have been quite commonplace in its day and not charged with any specific burden of extra suggestion or shock-meaning. Thus Douglas Bush, in an address given at the general meeting of the Modern Language Association in December 1948 ("The New Criticism: Some Old-Fashioned Queries," *PMLA,* LXIV, 1949), cited John Crowe Ransom's comment on Shakespeare's well-known lines "We are such stuff/ As dreams are made on," which draws extraordinary conclusions from the (to Mr. Ransom) odd use of *on* where we would say *of*—Shakespeare must have had an epiphenomenological view of consciousness or perhaps he wished to give an architectural cast to the dreams —and then pointed out, with examples, that "made on" was a common usage in Shakespeare's day to be found frequently elsewhere in Shakespeare and in other writers. Among other examples he also cited Mr. Ransom's puzzlement over the phrase *"dusty* death" in Macbeth's "Tomorrow and tomorrow and tomorrow" speech, when the phrase obviously came from the Bible and the burial service. (I give some other examples of this sort of thing in my discussion of American criticism of Yeats.)

We are back, on one level at least, to the fight between literary criticism and literary history—or rather, between literary criticism and history *tout court,* for it is history (a knowledge of the history of the language, the history of culture and of cultural habits) that supplies the necessary knowledge without which the critic is liable to talk nonsense. The critic has his reply: of course, he agrees, we must know what the text means, and we may have to go to history for a preliminary establishment of the text, just as we may have to go to the editor and bibliographer to tell us what the author really wrote or as we have to learn a foreign language before we can read a work in that language; but, he maintains, once that preliminary establishment of the text has been achieved, the critic is free to deal with the work of literary art as a work of literary art, not as a document in the history of ideas or in the biography of the author. To which in turn it might be answered that there is no single once-for-all establishment of the text in this sense. A continual sense of the writer's cultural context is necessary at every point in one's interpretation of an older work if we are not to be in danger of misreading. And so the argument goes on.

In fact, of course, many of those critics who pressed the claims of criticism as against history were themselves well read in history and in their analyses and interpretations continually employed, sometimes unconsciously, knowledge derived from their historical understanding—a knowledge they sometimes appeared to be denying to their pupils. Yet the whole controversy has been in a sense unreal. Eliot's insistence that poetry must be read as poetry and not another thing, an insistence reiterated by so many modern critics, leaves the question of the usefulness of historical knowledge in interpretation wholly open. A poem may still be regarded as a poem, a particular structure of meanings or however we choose to express it, even if we realize that to be sure that we really see what that particular structure of meanings is we must know something of the history of the language, the contemporary context of ideas, and so on. The historical critic has not argued that works of literary art should be read as documents in the history of ideas or in the biography of the author, as the "pure" critics have sometimes charged; he has rather argued that we must know the convention in which a given work is written and the meanings and suggestions possessed by words in a given time and place before we can read accurately. Thus no one has really disputed either that a work of literary art is a work of literary art or that one must be able to read the language in which it is written.

The most common charge of the historical critic is that the "pure" critic's ignorance of a particular convention or usage or tradition has led him to make an irresponsible and untenable interpretation of what a work *means*. There clearly have been occasions when such a charge was justified, even if such occasions have been fewer than the more polemic of the historical critics have suggested. Another charge that could be made, though in fact I have not seen it made at all often, is that a lack of reading *round* a particular work written in the past may disqualify a man's interpretation and judgment of it. I have myself interrogated a Ph.D. student who had written a thesis on a particular Jacobean dramatist and who was taken aback when it was suggested that he should know other Elizabethan and Jacobean dramatists than the one on whom he had done his research as well as nondramatic writers of the period. I also vividly recollect examining a Ph.D. candidate who had written a thesis on Carlyle's historiographical methods who was outraged when I asked him about the methods of Macaulay and Froude and Freeman and Green, none of

whom he had in fact read. Situations such as these are mani-
festations of the American vice of overspecialization in literary study, encouraged by the Ph.D. system and also by the
way in which courses are allotted to professors—one is an
early eighteenth century man or a Victorian novel man or
even a Spenser man or a Pope man. They are also connected
with the implication of so much modern criticism that one
can deal with a work of literature by confronting it directly
and nakedly and analyzing what one sees.

The "great books" idea, which was popular in Chicago
when I taught there, also in its own way encouraged this
view. I remember very clearly being asked to cooperate in
leading a "great books" discussion at Chicago. The topic was
the epistles of St. Paul, and the regular discussion leader
whom I joined for this occasion was pitiably ignorant of the
background of ideas with which St. Paul was working as well
as of the linguistic problems involved at some crucial points
so that, clever man though he was, he completely misled his
audience and in fact talked arrant nonsense. The "great
books" idea discouraged background reading: a great book
was a great book, and if a man knew "how to read a book" he
could tackle any example, however innocent he might be of
the intellectual background. There is of course a certain element of truth in this contention, but only an element, and in
any case much depends on the kind of book or work that is
being discussed. At the other extreme is the view once common among British classical scholars and forcefully stated by
that distinguished professor of Greek at St. Andrews, John
Burnet: "I would not give two straws for anyone's opinion on
the criticism or interpretation of Plato's text unless he can
write tolerable Greek prose" ("Humanism in Education," *Es-*

says and Addresses, 1924). I used to think of this remark of Burnet's when listening to Greek-less Chicago Aristotelians reinterpreting Aristotle with passion and sometimes with dogmatic violence.

Pressure to specialize; the influence of the New Critical notion that a critic needs to be trained in analysis rather than in the history of ideas and of modes of expression; and the "great books" idea that if a work is great it need only be confronted by a man who knows how to read, however ignorant he may be, for him to be able to read it with full understanding—all are factors helping to account for the fact that the run-of-the-mill American academic in the field of literature simply does not know enough. In the face of the enormous wealth of modern American literary scholarship this may seem a monstrous charge to bring, but I am not talking of the giants, nor am I talking of the sum of the parts of American scholarship; I am referring to the ordinary, not especially distinguished academic, who has sweated out his Ph.D. (the subject having been chosen for him by his professor) and become a reluctant expert in a phase of literature in which in all likelihood he never had any lively interest. These people often feel a professional obligation to keep up with the latest fashion in critical methodology but surprisingly little obligation to read widely in the whole field of the national literature that is their professional interest. This is perhaps less true of specialists in American literature, who are often called upon to teach survey courses in American literature (for this is an area where the survey course, having arrived latest, remains longest) and in any case the field of American literature is small compared with the whole field of English literature.

I know that most English departments require their Ph.D. students to show a wide range of reading before they are allowed to submit their theses, but I also know that this is often regarded as a terrible chore and that it rarely means the beginning of a habit of wide reading. Pressure of work, pressure to publish, and the particular kind of jadedness that seems to attack at some stage everyone who is professionally concerned with teaching an art such as literature are some of the reasons for this. The professor who reads "for pleasure" a light detective story of an evening, while reading genuine works of literary art only if he has to teach a course in them or make an article out of his reading, is a disturbing phenomenon of our time. How can the professional academic teacher of English literature preserve throughout the continuing daily chores of a long career that living interest, that genuine joy, in works of literature that presumably moved him originally to enter the profession?

Of course, those who did not originally choose the profession for this reason are not likely to see the problem. But many come to feel at some stage something analogous to what Coleridge records in his "Dejection Ode," a loss of joyous imaginative response, to be made up for by a weary ingenuity of explication. One cannot blame modern criticism for this; it is a danger inherent in the academic profession. The best minds emerge from this phase with renewed vigor, but there are many who never emerge, and there are many, too, who have been in this phase from the beginning. This is reflected, as much as anywhere, in the prose style of much critical and scholarly writing.

The richness of the American critical and scholarly scene is such that no sooner has one noted a trend than one be-

comes aware of its opposite. If an important element in modern American academic criticism refuses to discuss works of
literature as documents in the history of ideas because it
wishes to see them as poems or novels or plays to be read and
evaluated as such in accordance with the laws that govern the
nature of artistic expression and the unity of a work of art, it
is also true that some of the most significant work in the history of ideas has been done in America during the last thirty
years. Arthur O. Lovejoy's *The Great Chain of Being: A
Study in the History of an Idea,* first published in 1936, rapidly assumed the status of a classic. "In methodology, as well
as content, it has had immeasurable influence upon scholars
and students everywhere," Marjorie Hope Nicolson, who has
herself done distinguished work in this field, has commented.
In tracing the influence that a seminal idea has had upon cen-
turies of Western thought, Lovejoy developed a new kind of
intellectual history. He himself called the book "a contribution to the history of ideas," and went on to define this kind
of history.

> By a history of ideas I mean something at once more spe-
> cific and less restricted than the history of philosophy. It is
> differentiated primarily by the character of the unities with
> which it concerns itself. Though it deals in great part with
> the same material as the other branches of the history of
> thought . . . it divides that material in a special way, brings
> the parts of it into new groupings and relations, views it from
> the standpoint of a distinctive purpose.

That purpose was the quest of "unit-ideas" within the fluc-
tuating systems of philosophy; one result of such a quest,
Lovejoy maintained, would be "a livelier sense of the fact that

most philosophic systems are original or distinctive in their patterns rather than in their components." And indeed a lively sense of this fact has been shown by many recent American workers in this field (the *Journal of the History of Ideas* was founded in 1940). Lovejoy's *Essays in the History of Ideas* (1948), if it has not proved as germinal a book as *The Great Chain of Being,* has also had considerable influence.

Again, no sooner have we noted the tendency to overspecialize in American scholarship than we remember the interesting and illuminating work done by American scholars in bringing together science and literature. Marjorie Hope Nicolson's *Newton Demands the Muse: Newton's Opticks and the Eighteenth Century Poets* (1946) and her *The Breaking of the Circle: Studies in the Effect of the "New Science" on Seventeenth Century Poetry* (revised edition, 1960) are outstanding examples of a form of inquiry that now flourishes in several American universities. The third of Miss Nicolson's important trio of works is *Mountain Gloom and Mountain Glory: The Development of the Aesthetics of the Infinite* (1959), a contribution to the history of ideas and of sensibility of special interest to the literary student.

The *Journal of the History of Ideas* is two years older than *The Explicator* (1942 ff.) and in the long run is more influential. And it is worth noting that *Victorian Studies,* founded by a group of young scholars and critics at Indiana in 1957, is "a quarterly journal of the Humanities, Arts, and Sciences," bringing together articles on all aspects of Victorian life, thought, and art. In this connection it is not altogether irrelevant to note the increasing interest in the history of science in American universities. This is a "bridge subject" in itself and it is also a subject that can be of great interest to the student of literature. *Isis,* the quarterly journal of the History of Science Society, together with much that is of purely technical or specialist interest, contains articles that have been of real help to literary students.

The more we look into the matter the more it appears that in spite of the antihistorical implications of much modern American criticism, some of the most distinguished work done by American literary scholars today has been in the field of intellectual history. M. H. Abrams' *The Mirror and the Lamp* (1953), subtitled "Romantic Theory and Critical Tradition," examines and explains the significant changes that occurred in the early nineteenth century in the view of the nature and function of the work of literary art, setting the whole discussion firmly in a history-of-ideas context yet making its points by specific references to and subtle analyses of individual utterances by poets and critics. This book has justly been acclaimed as one of the finest achievements of modern American literary scholarship. It combines history of aesthetic theory, critical description and explanation, discussion of the relation between critical theory and creative practice, and a pervasive sense of the world of ideas inherited by and achieved by the writers whom it discusses. Abrams thus transforms the study of the sources and the consequences of certain notions about art into a total reinterpretation and revaluation of the romantic tradition in literature. The book shows clearly what romanticism moved away from, the conditions under which it moved and the direction in which it moved, and the significance and the results of the movement.

A further example of the prevalence of history in spite of everything is the massive *A Literary History of England* (1941) edited by Albert C. Baugh. This is not a one-man history; each period is dealt with by an expert: Kemp Malone, Baugh, Tucker Brooke, George Sherburn, and Samuel C. Chew are the contributors. Sherburn's section, "The Restoration and Eighteenth Century, 1660-1789," is one of the most impressive presentations of a period of literary history produced on either side of the Atlantic. It is interesting, too, that for one of the most difficult of all literary periods, the editors of the "Oxford History of English Literature" turned to an American scholar; Douglas Bush did the volume on *English Literature in the Earlier Seventeenth Century, 1600-1660* (1945), a work of scrupulous scholarship and controlled humanistic feeling. Bush is neither in the old Harvard philological tradition not in the new critical tradition. His sturdy common-sense conservatism, his classical knowledge, his dry wit, his respect for knowledge and contempt for ignorance, and the range of his literary interests (he has written on *Mythology and the Romantic Tradition in English Poetry* and *Science and English Poetry* as well as on *Mythology and the Renaissance Tradition in English Poetry*) add up to a highly individual character who suggests more an older type of British scholar than a contemporary American.

The revolt against history was primarily a revolt against the use of literary history *in teaching* as a substitute for reading the texts of individual literary works. It has, at least in the more sophisticated university English departments, virtually put an end to the old kind of potted survey course, and a good thing too. If it has also tended to discourage, at least among some students, that free reading around a text that alone can produce a full understanding of it, it cannot be said to have in any way interfered with the production of works on the history of ideas or with the application of the history of ideas to literary study, or indeed with the production of works of "pure" literary history. These latter activities have rather flourished with a new sophistication because of the increased self-consciousness about methodology that the debate has produced. Further, those who objected to the unhistorical freedom of interpretation claimed by some critics were driven to illustrate and bring home their objections by studies of the particular modes and traditions within which an earlier writer worked and with respect to which alone that writer can be fully understood. Rosamund Tuve's *Elizabethan and Metaphysical Imagery: Renaissance Poetic and Twentieth-Century Critics* (1947), Ruth Wallerstein's *Studies in Seventeenth-Century Poetic* (1950), and Louis L. Martz's *The Poetry of Meditation: A Study in English Religious Literature of the Seventeenth Century* (1954) are among the more interesting and helpful of those works that were written with this purpose in mind. This kind of study is now recognized as a characteristic modern American contribution to literary inquiry, and a most valuable one.

6

CRITICS AS TEACHERS

This is not the place for an extended study of the rise and significance of the New Criticism, but something must be said
of its impact on the American academic world. For, if there
have been quarrels in our time between scholars and critics,
this does not mean that the former speak for the universities
and the latter for the nonacademic world of periodical publication. The critics now belong to the university as much as
the scholars. Indeed, that is one reason why they sometimes
quarrel, since they find themselves advocating different ways
of doing the same thing. Nearly all the important literary
critics in America today are college professors, and even if
they are not they are very likely to have spent some time in
an academic institution as visiting professor (Kenneth Burke
and Edmund Wilson, for example, were both visiting professors at the University of Chicago during my time there.)
This bridging of the gap between the professor and the man
of letters is one of the most striking phenomena of modern
American culture. Poets and novelists too are drawn into the
academic orbit and are to be found as "poets in residence"
in liberal arts colleges or teaching "creative writing" courses
at universities. There are of course many reasons for this,
some of them economic, but to the European eye it appears as
(among other things) an example of the characteristic
American view that *everything* can be taught and that one
only has to have taken a course in something to be able to do

it. Literary courses at American colleges and universities range, one might say, from "How to read a book" to "How to write a book."

Something has already been said about the modern American critic's insistence on the differentiating qualities of a work of literary art and of his determination to find a way of describing literature in wholly nonhistorical terms so that in the description these differentiating qualities can be brought to light and concentrated on. Pedagogically, this means training the student to analyze the individual work, and techniques of analysis have in fact been developed further in America than in any other country. (It is true, and it has often been remarked, that such techniques bear some resemblance to the traditional French method of *explication de texte,* but the similarity is superficial: the kind of analysis to be found, for example, in Cleanth Brooks's account of Wordsworth's sonnet "Composed upon Westminster Bridge" is very different from the more rhetorical analysis one finds in French textbooks.)

If the concern is to train the student in criticism as well as to practice it, there must always be a conscious awareness of methodology or even a polemical insistence on one kind of methodology rather than another. Students—most of all it seems to me, American students—want to be taught *how to do it;* they want to learn the tricks of the trade. The critic, once he finds himself in the classroom, in spite of himself becomes involved in teaching the tricks of the trade to his students. The result is that often, instead of the critic dwelling with loving particularity on every aspect of a particular work that makes it that particular work—which is what he proclaims he is doing—he will make his criticism serve as a demonstration that his kind of criticism can really be applied to any work at all.

In his essay, "The Language of Paradox" (*The Well Wrought Urn,* 1947), Cleanth Brooks maintains that "there is a sense in which paradox is the language appropriate and inevitable to poetry" and goes on to show that this is as true of poems by Wordsworth as of poems by Donne. The paradoxes, ambiguities, complexes of attitudes, ambivalences, and similar characteristics that Brooks seeks in poetry are seen as belonging to poetry as such (the distinction is really between poetry as such and nonpoetry rather than between good and bad poetry, though this is never clearly brought out) so that once a work is seen as poetry it must either be shown to possess these characteristics or else be thrown out. Therefore if we are to admire properly a poem of Tennyson, even that must be shown to be susceptible to such an analysis—which Brooks duly provides in his discussion of "Tears Idle Tears" ("The Motivation of Tennyson's Weeper" in *The Well Wrought Urn*). My concern here is not to argue the merits of Brooks's analyses—some of which seem to me to be brilliant and others to be quite perverse—but to draw attention to the fact that they tend to be programatic, to mingle the manifesto and the illustration; they show in short how the thing can (and should) be done. This is not to say that Brooks insists that his own interpretations are uniquely right; indeed, he has grown more modest with the years and his later utterances are surprisingly tentative; but it *is* to maintain that Brooks is operating as a teacher, both urging and maintaining a particular method.

What is wrong, it might be asked, with the critic's operating as a teacher? Is this not his duty, particularly if he is in fact a university teacher? Every critic operates in some degree as a teacher. The danger surely lies in the (conscious or unconscious) insistence on a particular formula, thus suggesting that once one has mastered the formula one can produce similar acceptable critiques by its more or less routine application. I do not believe that any impartial observer of the American academic scene can say that this danger is imaginary. One of the saddest features of the mass of contemporary American academic criticism is precisely that it is formula-ridden, that it sets out to find the acquired ambiguities or whatever it is in the work under discussion, and of course by hook or by crook does eventually find them. The whole thing becomes a dogged exercise with no relation at all to any spontaneous and genuine appreciation of the work by the critic. With the livelier and more original minds, of course, this is not so; one sometimes finds evidence of a real excitement in a critic's demonstration of complexity of structure or a special kind of irony. But one consequence of America's huge (on European standards) numbers of colleges and universities is that there are not nearly enough lively and original minds to go round, and the dull dogs who plod their way year after year through their routine teaching chores must make their periodic burst into print and do so with a mechanical application of what they conceive to be the "method" to some work they happen to have had to teach. The result is generally worthless, and sometimes worse—dangerous. There are kinds of critical exercises that are useful *as* exercises, even if they are in themselves of no value, any more than the products of the student's chemistry experiment are of value in themselves, though they have helped to train the practitioner. But the product of a chemistry experiment is flushed down the sink once the experiment is over, not exhibited to an admiring audience of fellow academics as evidence of original powers. To publish a mechanical exercise in a method as criticism in its own right is to jeopardize the whole position of criticism both as a university study and as an activity in our culture.

The pedantic *Einfluss* hunter who fills the learned periodicals with meaningless evidence of assumed influence of X on Y, though he has far from disappeared, is no longer the characteristic example of academic sterility. His place has been taken by the critical pedant, who is more dangerous because he is supposed to be demonstrating why a poem or a novel or a play is important, why literature is a central part of our culture. I remember a bright if naïve student at an American university, who arrived from the South with a passion for poetry but little critical training, observing to me sadly after having heard an ingenious but wholly barren analysis of a couple of poems by a determined but far from brilliant practitioner of the New Criticism "I thought I liked poetry, but I see now that that was because I didn't know what it was." To be fair, I should also record another occasion at a Scottish university when a lecturer gave, before an audience of foreign teachers of English, a purely historical explanation of the imagery of a poem by Donne, an explanation so utterly removed from any literary awareness and so miserably pedantic in its dead detail, that it totally killed the poem for its audience, one of whom remarked to me afterward that up till then he had always thought the poem very fine, but he now saw that he had misread it! (The poem was "The Good Morrow.") There is more than one way of turning people away from literature.

The teaching of a particular kind of new critical analysis

has, it has been urged, taught a generation to *read,* and it is certainly true that the modern literary student is forced to pay detailed attention to the text. We can see the consequences almost everywhere in the published work of academics. There was a time when the characteristic academic essay on a writer or a work or a group of works was written on the assumption that the reader had not read or did not need to read the works discussed. Today it is difficult to find a serious discussion of a writer that does not take for granted that the reader has read the texts being discussed or that he will read them as he reads the discussion. To turn again to the 1907 volume of *PMLA* which I used before in comparing earlier work done on De Quincey with more recent work, one can find in that volume an article by William E. Bohn on "The Sources and Development of John Dryden's Literary Criticism" that consists very largely of a summary of Dryden's critical essays, in chronological order, so obviously intended for the reader who has not read those essays that in discussing the "Essay of Dramatic Poesy" Bohn actually tells the reader (as an item of information merely) that it is written in dialogue form. No such article would be accepted by an American learned journal or critical periodical today. This represents an undoubted gain. Yet a technique of close reading unrelated to a genuine sensitivity to literary value can in itself be of no more significance than a skill in doing crossword puzzles.

Can we blame the critics for the work of their more mechanical disciples? Is not any method liable to abuse? One can answer the former question in the negative and still be uneasily aware that a method of close analysis almost aggressively displayed in the classroom as an example of the right way of discussing a work of literature is bound to be an invitation to mere cleverness.

One of the paradoxes involved in much modern critical analysis of poetry is that amid all the concern with imagery— its meaning, its ordering, its total pattern of significance— there is remarkably little concern with the particular language in which the image is conveyed. For example, most readers of Wordsworth's sonnet "It is a beauteous evening calm and free" are struck by the unusual word *beauteous.* Is it there simply because *beautiful* has a syllable too many for the scansion? Is its literariness *used* in the poem, and if so how? How would the poem be worse if the line were "It is a lovely evening, calm and free?" Certainly not a single word of Brooks's discussion of the poem would have to be changed if *lovely* replaced *beauteous,* yet surely the poem would have suffered grievously.

Suppose we rewrote Gray's "Elegy" in a different stanza form, merely leaving out one foot in each line, thus:

> *The curfew tolls the knell of day,*
> *The herds wind slowly o'er the lea,*
> *The ploughman homeward wends his way,*
> *And leaves the darkening world to me.*

What is lost here besides the (perhaps unnecessary?) adjectives omitted in each line? What is the significance of the *tempo* of the stanza used by Gray? I know of no modern critical analysis of the "Elegy" that would have to be changed in any respect at all to be applicable to the stanzas rewritten as I have rewritten the first one. One of my own pedagogical techniques in teaching an "Introduction to the Criticism of Poetry" is to read a poem, then read very slowly a well-known modern analysis of it, then read my own rewriting of the poem (deliberately bad) to which nevertheless *everything said in the modern analysis is still applicable.*

The conclusion follows inevitably that whether what the analytic critic sees in the poem is really there or not his analysis does not contain the reasons why it is a good poem. But it is the reasons why it is a good poem that the student wants—or should want—to know.

The modern critic flees from what Brooks has called "the heresy of paraphrase." In Brooks's words: "The poem, if it be a true poem, is a simulacrum of reality—in this sense at least, it is an 'imitation'—by *being* an experience rather than any mere statement about experience or any mere abstraction from experience." ("The Heresy of Paraphrase," in *The Well Wrought Urn.*) In MacLeish's well-known echo of this modern view, "a poem should not mean but be." Yet in fact the modern critic's analysis often depends wholly on a special kind of paraphrase and often ignores qualities in the poet's use of language that are an essential part of the "being" of the poem.

The fact remains that adequate criticism cannot be taught by exhibiting a method with examples; it is the product of wide and sensitive reading, of that ability to hear the full harmony of meaning in a literary work that comes only from long and varied listening. "Taste"—the sum of all the discriminations that one has learned to make in the long continued cultivation of awareness—is still necessary, and no work can be adequately judged by a reader who knows that work alone. In his necessary and valuable reaction against vague impressionist chat and historical generalizations about literature the modern American critic, in his capacity as academic teacher, has tended to forget that perceptive reading and proper appraisal of literary works cannot be achieved by methodology alone and that the most important thing is continued exposure to literature. The kind of tact that knows when to press a meaning home and follow up all its possible implications and when it is absurd to do more than accept the primary meaning of an image, together with the historical understanding, derived from reading in different periods, that recognizes the area of suggestion that is relevant and appropriate to a given kind of expression—these are prerequisites for the proper practice of the art of criticism, prerequisites too often ignored by modern American criticism.

It is interesting to note that American students at Cambridge (England) who have in recent years gone there after graduating from an American university in order to read Part II of the English Tripos often surpass their British contemporaries in the brilliance and sophistication of their critical analyses. But there is one question in the "practical criticism" paper in which they almost invariably do badly. That is the "dating" question in which the student is presented with a series of anonymous extracts of prose and poetry and asked to assign them to their proper period by using whatever internal evidence seems appropriate (style, tone, vocabulary, sensibility, subject matter, and so forth). Set the good American student to write an essay on varieties of irony in a James novel and he will produce something quite sparkling; ask him to place in their periods ten unidentified lines by Waller and ten by Edward Thomas and he is at a loss. Or again, give him two good poems and ask him to discuss them and he will produce extremely interesting analyses, but give him one good and one indifferent poem (both unidentified) without telling him that they are not both good, and the same sparkling demonstration of ambiguities and so on will be produced for both. Tell him that one is good and one bad, and he will more often than not find his analytic skills useless in deciding which is which.

The modern American student, it seems, is not taught to discriminate; he is taught to demonstrate quality by analysis, on the assumption that what is set before him is of good quality. Except for a few stock examples ("Trees," and some of the more gushing examples of romantic poetry), he is presented with works already determined by tradition to be "good" or "great" and has then to prove this goodness or greatness by demonstrating the proper kind of texture and structure. I once lectured to a very sophisticated young academic audience in New York and in the course of the lecture presented for their analysis (without revealing its authorship) a poem I had composed over breakfast that morning that was just a jumble of free association with some echoes from Eliot and Yeats. Not one single member of the audience said that the poem was nonsense (as it was); each was prepared to work at his analysis until he had demonstrated its complex pattern.

Having said all this, I must present the other side of the picture. In spite of the foregoing remarks, I believe that it is indisputable that modern American criticism is the most interesting, the most fruitful, and the most exciting in the English speaking world today, and that the galaxy of critics that includes such names as John Crowe Ransom, Kenneth Burke, Edmund Wilson, Richard Blackmur, Allen Tate, Lionel Trilling, Robert Penn Warren, and Cleanth Brooks cannot be easily matched in any other time or place. Some of those in this list are in the strict sense "new" critics, if by "new" we mean those committed to the kind of critical analysis made so popular in American colleges and universities by Brooks and Warren's very widely used anthology *Understanding Poetry* (1938), but each is new in the sense that he has something interesting and original to say.

Ransom's "Poetry: A Note in Ontology" (1934), in spite of the pretentiousness of its title and its somewhat wilful terminology, is one of the most provocative and stimulating essays on poetry of the century, and has had great influence; Allen Tate's essay "Tension in Poetry" (1938) contributed to the criticism of poetry a new concept and a new term that have been in continuous use ever since; Richard Blackmur's essay on "The Shorter Poems of Thomas Hardy" (1940) is the finest existing treatment of its subject and a classic of its kind; Robert Penn Warren's "Pure and Impure Poetry" (1943)—which I would give to read to anybody brought up on *The Golden Treasury* who wanted to understand what lies behind the modern change in poetic taste—is a brilliantly argued and cunningly illustrated treatment of some of the fundamental presuppositions of modern poetic theory and practice.

And so one could go on. It is to be noted that most of these critics are at the same time either poets or novelists *and* academic teachers. Here is a coming together of criticism, creation, and teaching that represents something new in the academic world, something pioneered by America. Amid all the overspecialization and fragmentation that are going on in our culture, here is a movement in the other direction. And this movement goes a long way toward counteracting the effect of what might be called overmethodologizing that I have already discussed.

The intellectual gaiety that so finely aerates Robert Penn Warren's criticism is surely bound up in some way with his being himself both poet and novelist as well as critic and teacher. One senses the creative mind at play as well as the teacher at work. (This is one reason why Brooks, brilliant though he can be, never quite has Warren's appeal; Brooks is a critic and teacher but not a poet or novelist.) When Blackmur illustrates a point about one of Hardy's poems by showing how a later poet might have rearranged it, he is using his instinct as a poet to reinforce and illustrate his insights as a critic. Similarly, Tate's best criticism clearly reflects the kind of awareness that he has developed as a creative writer. Indeed, it can be said in general that criticism and creation have moved closer together in modern America than they ever have anywhere else before.

T. S. Eliot, in his essay "The Function of Criticism" (1923), made a point that has seemed especially relevant to an important area of modern American writing: "Probably . . . the larger part of the labour of an author in composing his work is critical labour; the labour of sifting, combining, constructing, expunging, correcting, testing: this frightful toil is as much critical as creative. I maintain even that the criticism employed by a trained and skilled writer on his own work is the most vital, the highest kind of criticism. . . ." This is congenial doctrine to the best kind of modern American academic critic, who tends to see the critical faculty as very closely associated with the creative.

If there is an earnest, dogged application of the received

technique in a large amount of run-of-the-mill criticism coming out of American universities today, there is also a considerable quantity of imaginative and adventurous critical writing that combines analytic rigor with intellectual boldness. This boldness can be irresponsibility; it can result in fancy games of intellectual hide-and-seek or in the invention or adaptation of scores of fantastic new technical terms or in a kind of scholastic gymnastics that is sometimes hard to take seriously. But often it produces something genuinely fresh and stimulating, immensely exhilarating to someone who comes from an older academic tradition of either elegant generalization or textbook formulation. Critics like Blackmur and Trilling and Brooks—very different from each other— are being increasingly discovered in Europe with enormous excitement. It is true that many of the characteristics of modern American criticism represent developments of attitudes found in Eliot, Richards, and others who wrote in England (a recent University of Nebraska study in "The New Critics and the Language of Poetry," by C. E. Pulos, deals only with Ford Madox Ford, T. E. Hulme, Ezra Pound, T. S. Eliot, I. A. Richards, William Empson, and Cleanth Brooks), but the developments have been original and significant, and the work of the New Critics is received abroad for the most part as something American and new.

The Chicago school's rediscovery and reinterpretation of Aristotle is but one of several examples of a new and original use of classical and even of medieval writers in order to develop new critical techniques or to modify old ones. While on the one hand the decline of a living classical tradition in American education means a loss of an adequate reading knowledge of Latin and Greek among educated people, even among university teachers (who are not professors of Classics), on the other hand it means that those who do turn to the Latin and Greek classics do so with freshness and enthusiasm, unjaded by years of conventional drill. Some of the freshest work done on Greek drama today is being done in America for this reason, and among the few American scholars who are competent in Greek are poets and critics who have produced admirable translations of Greek plays (one thinks of Dudley Fitts, Richmond Lattimore, and Robert Fitzgerald).

The study of Greek tragedy is compulsory in Part II of the Cambridge English Tripos and it is surprising how many of the students now depend on American sources—translations and critical works—in preparing for their examination in this subject. The interest in myth and symbol and allegory that has developed from the study of classical and medieval literature has been applied by many critics to enlarge their view of literature and to enrich their critical vocabulary. Anyone reading Francis Fergusson's *The Idea of a Theatre* (1949) or Blackmur's collection of essays, *Language as Gesture* (1952), can see how a new kind of curiosity about classical and medieval literature is working in the critic's whole intellectual approach. In a critic such as Trilling (or, in a different way, Edmund Wilson) we get something else characteristically American—a view of European culture *as a whole* that Europeans, living in the midst of it, rarely possess.

This again is in sharp contrast to the trend of overspecialization already discussed. Here we have critics who move from *Piers Plowman* to Stendhal, from Dante to Verlaine, from Virgil to Rilke, with a provocative comparison, an urbanely suggested analogy, a suppressed quotation or implied allusion. This kind of critic is not involved in the complexities and scholasticisms of the typical New Critic, or at least rarely involved (Trilling occasionally goes in for this sort of thing); their characteristic attitude is one of humanist concern with the ways in which literature renders the human condition. In a brief description such as this, this may sound rather the Victorian "Musings among my Books" species of criticism, but it is in fact very unlike. An awareness of all the subtleties of New Critical analysis lies behind their most casual-seeming utterance and the whole texture of their thought and expression is thoroughly tough.

Critical discourse is difficult: that is one of the implied maxims of modern American academic criticism. It is difficult, because to tell the exact truth about the way a work of literature is organized, about the total pattern of significance that it comprehends, involves precise and delicate chartings of meaning. Many critics seem to believe that because adequate critical discourse is difficult, any critical discourse that is difficult is thereby shown to be adequate, and this may account for the amount of unnecessary difficulty, of sheer ungainliness, in much modern American critical writing. On the other hand, there is a tendency among British observers of the American academic scene to assume too readily that a facile urbanity of style is necessarily the best kind of style for the literary critic. There is a kind of ruggedness that is the inevitable result of a critic's really trying to come to grips with his subject, being wholly honest in his insights and unsparing in his attempts to record and account for them accurately. Difficulty of style can be the mark of genuine originality and profundity (no one had a less elegant prose style than Coleridge) and a charming lucidity may simply indicate superficiality. This is not of course always true, and is probably less true than many serious American critics today believe. Kenneth Burke, at his best a truly brilliant critic, is surely sometimes grotesque and pretentious in vocabulary and expression. Philip Wheelwright, poet and philosopher as well as literary critic, can, even in his most illuminating work, break into the most intolerable and sometimes actually meaningless jargon. I have compiled (but will refrain from publishing) a list of misused Greek words employed by some of the most distinguished contemporary American critics. But all this is evidence of a genuine intellectual ferment. There are more *ideas* concerning literature in America today than there have been, I suspect, in the whole of American history.

Interest in myth and symbol has reached enormous proportions in contemporary America. On the one hand it has grown out of the kind of study related to Jungian psychology that first found expression in England in Maud Bodkin's *Archetypal Patterns in Poetry* (1934), or out of the anthropological literary interests of the English poet Robert Graves (*The White Goddess,* 1947; *The Greek Myths,* 1955). On the other hand it has grown independently out of a realization that American fiction, particularly the great novelists of the nineteenth century (Melville, Hawthorne) works with symbolic landscapes rather than with a fully differentiated class-patterned social scene. It was Trilling who first made the point that while the English novelist is socially grounded and obsessed with class, American fiction, lacking a stable and long-continued class structure against which to set human relationships and develop moral patterns, has tended to make its characters into symbolic figures divorced from any intimate contact with time and place who act out their violent and unresolved dilemmas against what is virtually a cosmic background.

The thesis has been widely accepted, and indeed lies behind Richard Chase's book, *The American Novel and Its Tradition* (1957). Its acceptance has encouraged the quest for myth and symbol in fiction. We find American critics, with tools derived from an analysis of the symbolic patterns in Melville, Hawthorne, and Faulkner, turning to Dickens or Conrad or Joyce and making them, as it were, into American novelists, to the surprise and sometimes the indignation of English academics. Of course, both Conrad and Joyce were very much interested in the symbolic aspects of fiction, and even Dickens probably incorporated more deliberately symbolic elements into his work than he admitted or than his readers suspected. Nevertheless, we do have the feeling, in reading *Charles Dickens: The World of His Novels* by J. Hillis Miller (1958), for example, that, for all the book's genuine perceptiveness and original insights, Miller is rather making Dickens into a Melville.

At any rate, the search for myth and symbol—in fiction, in poetry, in Shakespearean drama—has been for some years now an American preoccupation. There are clear traces of it in Brooks and Warren's *Understanding Fiction* (1943), in many of Blackmur's essays, in the work of Leslie Fiedler, and in many other critics. Richard Chase's *Quest for Myth* (1949), William York Tindall's *The Literary Symbol* (1955), and Philip Wheelwright's *The Burning Fountain: A Study in the Language of Symbolism* (1954) are central documents in the myth-and-symbol movement. W. H. Auden, who must now be regarded as an American academic critic in spite of his English background and his having held the Oxford Chair of Poetry, produced in *The Enchafèd Flood: or, The Romantic Iconography of the Sea* (1950: originally lectures delivered at the University of Virginia in 1949), a characteristically lively and stimulating inquiry into sea symbolism in nineteenth century literature, European and American. And the brilliant and highly influential work of the Canadian critic Northrop Frye must be mentioned here: his *Anatomy of Criticism* (1957), an ambitious and fascinating study that shows how to place a given work of literature by defining its mode, its kind and degree of symbolization, the kind of archetypal themes and images it employs, and the way it handles words with respect to a real or implied audience or to the writer's relationship to his material, already shows signs of becoming something of a bible to the new generation of critics concerned with myth and symbol. This line of interest has produced much that is illuminating, much that is provocative, and a fair amount that is wholly absurd. Like so many movements in modern American criticism, it lends itself easily to unconscious parody, and when the search for myth and symbol gets out of hand it can yield some pretty fancy nonsense. When there are so many people waiting for the word about what and how to write, it is difficult for any technique not to be overdone almost as soon as it appears.

No account of the American critic as academic teacher would be remotely adequate without some mention of that graduate student's vade mecum, *Theory of Literature* (1949), by René Wellek and Austin Warren. Here, in a single volume, is a carefully organized presentation of all that the student concerned with the methodology of literary study needs to know. The authors themselves define the book as an "attempt to formulate the assumptions on which literary study is conducted." The chapter entitled "Image, Metaphor, Symbol, Myth" opens: "When we turn from classifying poems by their subject matter or themes to asking what kind of discourse poetry is, and when, instead of prose-paraphrasing, we identify the 'meaning' of a poem with its whole complex of structures, we then encounter, as central poetic structure, the sequence represented by the four terms of our title." There are chapters on "The Nature of Literature," "The Function of Literature," "Literature and Psychology," "Literature and Society," "Literature and Ideas," "The Analysis of the Literary Works of Art," "The Nature and Modes of Narrative Fiction," among others. All the sophistication of modern criticism lies behind this modern critical *Summa*. The British reader tends to bridle at this kind of sustained theoretical discussion, holding that an ounce of practice is worth a pound of theory and that criticism, to be useful, should be concrete. But the work is a truly remarkable feat of presentation and systematization, maintaining a high level of philosophic discourse and being intellectually scrupulous in the highest degree. At what point in the student's study of literature the work ought to be studied is clearly a debatable question: it might be argued that much of it does not belong in the literature classroom at all, but in the philosophy classroom.

Wellek is also responsible for an ambitious *History of Modern Criticism, 1750-1950,* of which the first two volumes have so far appeared (1955). Wellek's remarkably wide range of reading, his knowledge of European languages (including the Slavic), and his thorough philosophical competence make him unusually well qualified to write such a work. He is not a relativist, nor is he content to expound every critic and leave it at that; he is continually assessing the degree to which a particular critic contributed to our mature modern view of literature, and he gives praise or blame according to whether a critic points forward or leads away from the position developed in *Theory of Literature*. But this is not a polemical work, rather a work guided by a deep sense of contemporary relevance. There is probably no critic writing in America today who is as learned as Wellek and who has at the same time been so deeply immersed in the controversies of modern criticism. His article on "Literary Theory, Criticism, and History" (*Sewanee Review,* 1960) is only one of many evidences of his active concern with the major critical problems that have agitated critics in our time. Its conclusion is interesting: "We must return to the task of building a literary theory, a system of principles, a theory of values which will necessarily draw on the criticism of concrete works of art and will constantly invoke the assistance of literary history. But the three disciplines are and will remain distinct: history cannot absorb or replace theory, while theory should not even dream of absorbing history. . . ."

A more comprehensive history of literary criticism, in one volume, has been written by William K. Wimsatt Jr. and Cleanth Brooks, *Literary Criticism: A Short History* (1957). Each of these two authors is a distinguished critic in his own right, and it is significant that after producing much original work they have turned to a reinterpretation of the criticism of the past. It is a genuine reinterpretation, in which the views of each writer are treated with an absorbed scrupulousness that seems to have learned something from the analysis of poems and novels. It is more deliberately objective than Wellek's work, for it is not concerned to chart the development of a movement and to give marks to each critic in proportion to the degree of help he gives in making goal. It is, however, written from a point of view (as all history that is not mere chronicling must be); comparisons are made, but not before each view has been probed to reveal its inner pattern and its relation to the world of creation that surrounded it, and everything is done with a sense of modern relevance and modern needs. So in spite of all the attacks on history, we come back to history in the end.

7

BIOGRAPHY AND LETTERS

Modern American literary scholarship has been conspicu-
ously successful in the field of biography. This is partly because many biographers have been able to get substantial
awards from one or other of the great American foundations
to enable them to pursue their researches in peace of mind
and on the spot. Edgar Johnson's *Charles Dickens: His Tragedy and Triumph* (2 vols., 1952), Gordon Ray's two volumes on Thackeray (*The Uses of Adversity, 1811-1846,*
1955; *The Age of Wisdom, 1847-1863,* 1958), Leslie A.
Marchand's *Byron: A Biography* (3 vols., 1957), Ernest C.
Mossner's *Life of David Hume* (1954) are works of exact
scholarship, done with careful attention to detail, each the
product of long and intensive research. Sometimes in biographies such as these we may feel that we cannot see the forest
for the trees, and that we would be ready to sacrifice some of
the scrupulous documentation for a briefer account that
would body forth with greater vividness the essential quality
of the subject. But this would be to demand a very different
kind of work. The objective of modern scholarly biography is
to record, with a proper indication of the sources, everything that can be found out about the subject's life and be-
havior. This is not the pious "authorized biography" that the
Victorians went in for (Buckle and Monypenny's six-volume
Life of Disraeli, for example), nor is it the more personal
"interpretative" account of a man that is still commoner now

in Britain than in America (Betty Miller's *Robert Browning: A Portrait,* for example). It is written as a rule with a studied objectivity, and is often more likely to be used as a work of reference than to be read straight through. Many modern American biographies have corrected errors that have persisted for generations.

Another factor in the production of such biographies, in addition to the help given by foundations, is the accumulation in American university libraries of letters and other original sources. Sometimes a scholar working at a particular university has a virtual obligation to write a book in order to make conspicuous use of the material available in the library; the presence of such material certainly provides unique opportunities for scholars to do original research. A whole reputation can be based on the lucky presence of invaluable source material in the library of the institution where a scholar is working.

An editorial in the (London) *Times Literary Supplement* of 30 June 1961 pointed out that the recent trend toward collecting manuscripts and other materials by living authors has replaced the collection of first editions that boomed in the late 1920's, and attributed this trend to "American institutional appetites." Commenting on this editorial, Mr. David Randall, Librarian at the University of Indiana, pointed out in the issue of 11 August that "unlike the private collector, gratifying his own whims, the directors of libraries, many fairly new to the collecting game and striving to build 'resources,' often find it difficult to justify to a board of directors, or a faculty committee, acquisition of the originals of printed works readily available in facsimiles, scholarly edited editions, etc. It is equally difficult," Mr. Randall's letter went on, "to justify the purchase of published letters or ad hoc transcripts of manuscripts for other than purely exhibition purposes. However, purchasing 'archives,' with reams of unpublished material, grist for the Ph.D. (or the professor) avid for publication or publicity, can be easily defended as needed 'research material.' And possibly quite rightly. A university must attempt to acquire source material which will interest its scholars or risk losing them to those who have such resources."

The discussion in the *Times Literary Supplement* referred to collection of material by modern writers, but Mr. Randall's arguments apply equally to older material. The Boswell material at Yale, the Thackeray material at Illinois, the Joyce material at Cornell, the wealth of workbooks by modern writers at the Lockwood Memorial Library at Buffalo (including the invaluable Wickser and Sylvia Beach Collections of Joyce manuscripts, notebooks, and so forth) and the Conrad manuscripts in the Keating collection at Yale are only a few examples of important original material that has been used by American scholars. The Yale "Boswell factory" is perhaps a rather special case—it certainly gives employment to more graduate students than any other collection I am aware of—but it may not long remain so. The accumulation of manuscript material for the study of English writers is proceeding apace in American universities; more and more collections find their way across the Atlantic, and English scholars working on one of their native writers often have to spend some time working in America on essential material. The H. G. Wells Archive at the University of Illinois has already resulted in three books (Wells's correspondence with Henry James, Arnold Bennet, and George Gissing respectively) that have justified, in Mr. Randall's sense as well as in others, the university's purchase of the collection.

Editions of letters stand beside biographies as a major modern American contribution. The thirty-one volumes so far published of Horace Walpole's correspondence, edited by W. S. Lewis (1937 ff.), Gordon Ray's *Letters and Private Papers of W. M. Thackeray* (4 vols., 1945-46), Gordon S. Haight's *George Eliot Letters* (7 vols., 1954-56), and Cecil Y. Lang's already published four volumes of his projected six of *The Swinburne Letters* (1959 ff.) are such fully (and often over-fully) annotated collections that they have raised the question whether such mammoth enterprises do not in the end defeat themselves by providing more material than can ever be relevant for a full understanding of the writer and his work.

It can be argued that the scholar who has set himself the task of collecting and editing the letters of an important writer has a duty to preserve and annotate every single item he can lay his hands on, even the most trivial laundry bill or formal reply to an invitation to dinner; no one can say when some item, however, absurdly unimportant it may seem to any given reader, might not eventually turn out to be of some interest or some help. It might also be argued that even if some items could never conceivably be of any interpretative or critical or illustrative use they should still be collected if they can be found, for the scholar's aim is completeness. To which it may be replied that so long as the complete record is preserved somewhere, the production in book form of such detailed collections of letters and papers is unnecessary and indeed harmful, because it inevitably puts the price of the book beyond the means of the private reader, so that as a rule it will be bought only by libraries, and also because it is likely to prevent any but the most specialized of scholars from reading it through. A collection of a writer's letters, it might well be urged, is or should be intended to be an illumination of the writer's life and personality to be read as such by the general reader or at least by the reader with some professional interest in literature, not only by a handful of experts. Again one could reply that this is the function of *another* kind of editing—the kind of editing that aims at the kind of completeness here envisaged has another purpose, namely the publication and perpetuation of the total record. Such a book, it could be maintained, belongs on the library shelves rather than in the private home. One can take a position on either side of this argument; the fact remains that there is a tendency in all fields of literary scholarship and even of criticism to write for the fellow expert only and this, however inevitable it may be in modern conditions, cannot be regarded as healthy.

The Wells letters already referred to have been brought out in three small, attractive books and are obviously designed to interest the more-or-less general reader—as indeed they seem to have done. And there are some letter writers whose letters are always a joy to read, in however large a bulk. This applies to Robert Louis Stevenson, a complete edition of whose letters has never yet been published, although a near-complete edition is, at the time of writing, in the process of being produced by Bradford A. Booth. Stevenson's wonderfully entertaining letters to Charles Baxter were edited by J. DeLancey Ferguson and Marshall Waingrow in 1956. This is another example of a publication made possible by the presence in an American university library of a manuscript collection, in this case the splendid Beinecke Collection at Yale, which includes the important Savile Gift of Stevenson's letters to Baxter. Mr. Beinecke and his collection were also of the greatest help (this was immediately before Mr. Beinecke presented the collection to Yale) to J. C. Furnas in writing his definitive biography of Stevenson, *Voyage to Windward* (1951). This book is worth special mention because it is written not by a professor but by a professional journalist who spent several years following Stevenson's tracks and ferreting out information about him; in so doing he demonstrated that the techniques of the first-rate journalist are not significantly different from those of the scholar when it comes to what might be called the detective aspect of scholarship. Furnas's biography exploded many myths about Stevenson and solved several hitherto unsolved problems about him.

More and more it becomes clear that it is to American scholars that one must turn if one wants the full facts about an author—whether the author be Thackeray or Joyce, Boswell or D. H. Lawrence, Pope or H. G. Wells. James L. Clifford's biography of *Hester Lynch Piozzi* (*Mrs. Thrale*) (1941) and his *Young Samuel Johnson* (1955), George Sherburn's *Early Career of Alexander Pope* (1934), Franklyn B. Snyder's *Life of Burns* (1932), J. DeLancey Ferguson's two-volume edition of Burns's letters (1931), and George Healey's edition of Defoe's letters (1955)—I select almost at random from books on my own shelves—can be added to the other biographies and editions of letters mentioned as examples of works that show a degree of erudition and thoroughness of

137

treatment that make earlier English treatments of the same subject seem breezy and careless.

It must be remembered that American scholars are prepared in graduate school for the rigors of the scholarly life. They are taught to take nothing for granted, to be meticulous about their sources, to footnote fully and precisely, as well as to seek all over the world if necessary for relevant original material; whereas the British scholar has in all likelihood never had a course in anything since he took his B.A., and worked up his method himself. (Except at Oxford, British doctoral candidates do not take any courses, but simply write their theses.) When E. C. Mossner came from America to Edinburgh to work on David Hume he asked Professor Kemp Smith, the great Edinburgh authority on Hume, whether there was any possibility of finding new Hume letters, at which Kemp Smith laughed and made some remark about the incorrigible optimism of Americans. But in fact Mossner did find many new Hume letters, and Americans in Britain, by their sheer doggedness, have several times turned up new source material that the British scholar has never bothered to hunt down. (The most famous case of all is of course that of the Boswell papers at Malahide.) The Ph.D. system, the pressure to research and publish, the buying of source material by American university libraries, and the generosity of the great American foundations together add up to the fact that in certain areas of scholarship America is supreme. American scholars have the facts. Whether they always see them in proper perspective or present them with proper persuasiveness or interpret them with complete understanding is another question. In many cases they do; many of the biographies cited above are admirable for more than their naked scholarship. In many other cases the work produced is more useful for reference than for reading in any humane sense.

⤳ 8 ⤶

THE INDUSTRIOUS SCHOLAR

The rise in the academic prestige of criticism, which was one of the consequences of making criticism a strenuous discipline in its own right, has not meant the disappearance of the industrious American scholar who still is, or can be, together with the German scholar, the most industrious in the world. The meticulous piling up of card indexes can, and sometimes does, become obsessive. I know personally of at least one important American project that got crushed under the weight of hundreds of thousands of index cards; after some twenty years of work the intention of using the material in a book was finally abandoned. I found as a professor in America that graduate students had to be restrained from accumulating enormous quantities of references on cards and set to writing up the meaning of their findings before they became paralyzed by the material they had amassed. A favorite way of beginning a thesis was to compile an unrealistically large bibliography of every conceivable book and article remotely connected with the subject—and then the student wondered what to do next. Students of literature should realize from the beginning that a large part of what has been written on any literary subject is liable to be nonsense and learn to be less in awe of the bibliographical item. Now that electronic computers can provide aids beyond the scope of the card index, and with unprecedented speed, one wonders what new kinds of accumulation will emerge. Recent reports of a computer at work on the *Iliad* and the *Odyssey* to identify and classify tricks of style and meter in order to solve the problem of single or multiple authorship suggest a variety of possibilities.

It is easy to mock mere industry, but mere industry has valuable uses to the literary scholar. The most recent Milton bibliography, Calvin Huckabay's *John Milton: A Bibliographical Supplement 1929-1957* (1960), with its nearly two thousand items, represents a formidable amount of labor, perhaps disproportionate to the amount of actual help the work will ever give to scholars and critics; but clearly one must know what has been written and where to find it. Huckabay's work is a supplement to the earlier Milton bibliographies, David H. Stevens' *Reference Guide to Milton from 1800 to the Present Day* (1930) and Harris Fletcher's *Contributions to a Milton Bibliography, 1800-1930* (1931); the total labor involved in all three works is formidable. Professor Hanford, in a private letter to me, after citing the help in finding a particular item that he received from Huckabay's bibliography, added: "Yet who would call even Dave Stevens' *Reference Guide* anything but a useful piece of slave labor in a good cause? I'm sure he would not." The phrase is a good one; "a useful piece of slave labor in a good cause" is what a considerable amount of scholarship inevitably is.

There was a time when in certain quarters that kind of slave labor, and only that kind, was regarded as true "research." Now, when Ph.D. theses are as likely to be critical and interpretative as "scholarly" in this restricted sense, the graduate student is free to range far more widely. This also means that he is free to write nonsense, and that is an obvious accompaniment of freedom to write. In Cambridge, where we have many applications from Americans to do research in English, we have sometimes been struck by the sheer oddness of a proposed topic—they have ranged from a study of gardens and children in English literature to the religious attitudes of George Moore. But the study of a freely chosen "nonsense subject" (as we are perhaps too ready to call some subjects in England) may be more rewarding than the plodding accumulation of factual material that requires no genuinely critical operation at all. There is sometimes a tendency to steer the less bright graduate student on to such a topic. I remember that when I was teaching at Chicago, one of my graduate students produced a critical thesis of distressingly inferior quality and one of my colleagues suggested that I advise him to produce a straight bibliography of his subject instead; this he did, and got his degree.

Somebody must do the donkey work, even in the age of the computer. The question is, should it be done by a sensitive and intelligent scholar, or by a harmless drudge? It is easy to say that the drudges can drudge and the scholar-critic can then make intelligent use of the results of the drudgery, but the situation is rarely as simple as this (though there are many fortunate professors in America today who have grants from a foundation to pay research students to look up their references and do their research drudgery). There is nearly always some point in the accumulation of knowledge relevant to literary scholarship where discrimination and literary judgment are necessary if even purely factual errors are to be avoided. And, it is often urged, every literary scholar should have some experience of the more grinding side of research so that he knows what is involved and thus becomes a better judge of others' efforts in that sphere.

There are of course distinctions to be made. There is, for example, the distinction between Browning's grammarian and the researcher who lists every case where London is mentioned in English literature; there is the distinction between the skilled bibliographer or paleographer or textual critic, who has to possess a great variety of learning and of technical skills and apply them with tact and discrimination, and the man who simply collects and lists variant readings and so on. The making of a concordance is generally, and with some reason, regarded as mere drudgery; but Lane Cooper at Cornell was a fervent believer in the usefulness of concordances, in helping the compiler as well as the user to get inside the mind of the author, and saw their making as contributing to a liberal education. Many concordances were compiled by his students under his inspiration. The electronic computer can now take over much of this kind of work—and presumably is the recipient of any liberal education that it brings.

In the field of bibliography the American scholar remains supremely industrious. There is scarcely an important (or even unimportant) writer whose bibliography has not been painstakingly compiled in the United States. And there are reader's guides of all sorts. The various bibliographies published in American learned journals (e.g., the eighteenth century bibliographies in the *Philological Quarterly* of which those from 1926 to 1950 appeared in two volumes in 1950-52, or the Victorian bibliographies that used to appear annually in *Modern Philology* and have recently been taken over by *Victorian Studies,* or the annual bibliographies, arranged in periods, in *PMLA*) are of the utmost value to anybody wishing to know what has been and is being done in particular fields, and have been of great help in the writing

---

◦§ 9 §◦

THE PAPERBACK REVOLUTION

The availability of many important works of literary scholarship and criticism in paperback editions represents a significant development in American education. Paperback editions are not only cheaper than clothbound editions but they are also more *buyable,* as it were, appealing to the reader as books to be bought and used rather than as formidable volumes intended for the university library. One finds serious works of criticism or well-edited texts of classics in bookstores and even drugstores cheek by jowl with detective stories and sensational popular fiction. I remember my surprise some years ago (it was my first realization of the importance of this new movement in publishing) to find in a Midwestern drugstore, among a great mass of rubbish and do-it-yourself manuals, paperbound editions of G. F. Kitto's *Greek Tragedy* and F. R. Leavis's *The Great Tradition.* These particular books do not happen to be by American writers, but the great majority of serious paperbacks available in America today are by Americans or edited by Americans.

In the latest quarterly catalog of *Paperbound Books in Print* available to me as I write (New York, Spring, 1961) there are listed a total of almost 3,000 works of direct interest to the student of literature. Of these, 149 are critical works on drama and collections of plays, 65 contain one or more Greek or Roman plays in translation, 171 contain an English play or plays (including over 80 volumes of single

of this essay. The guides to and reviews of research (e.g., *The English Romantic Poets: A Review of Research,* edited by T. M. Raysor, 1950; *The Victorian Poets: A Guide to Research,* edited by F. E. Faverty, 1956) are also characteristic American contributions.

All these lists and aids testify to the proliferation of scholarship in America, to its organized and indeed competitive nature. Literary research is a recognized function of American culture, planned and supervised in scores of universities, encouraged and financed by foundations established by businessmen. The competition is at one level between individuals (who have to produce research to get on in the profession) and at another, more and more, between institutions who organize teams to work on particular projects so that it becomes increasingly impossible to assess individual contributions.

American industriousness in literary scholarship is by no means confined to the compiling of bibliographies. The encyclopedic nature of Stith Thompson's listing, classifying, and identifying the motifs in the folk literature of the world (*Motif-Index of Folk-Literature,* 1932 ff.) is one example of a quite different kind of industriousness, while H. N. Fairchild's four volumes on *Religious Trends in English Poetry* (1939-57) are an example of an older kind of enterprise carried on into our period. Reference has already been made to the massive editions of annotated letters brought out by modern American scholars, and to some of the more laborious enterprises in Shakespeare and Milton scholarship. One could mention also the nine-volume variorum edition of Spenser edited by Greenlaw, Osgood, Padelford, and Heffner (1932-48). (It is interesting, incidentally, that all six items in the category "Bibliographies and Concordances" listed

under "Spenser" in *The Cambridge Bibliogr[aphy of English] Literature* are American. The Cambridge bib[liography,] it need hardly be added, is British.) There ar[e Rol-] lins' eight volumes of the *Pepys Ballads* [(1929-32),] together with his other work on ballads, his [*Paradise of Dain-] tel's Miscellany* and other Tudor miscellani[es, and the many] volumes of letters, papers, and poems of t[he period, which] constitute a remarkable achievement for a si[ngle scholar.]

Generalizations about different kinds of s[cholarship in a situa-] tion whose only common feature is the lab[or that went into it] and the bulk of resulting published work i[s clearly futile.] One could walk through the library stacks a[nd mention the] names of every American publication in t[he humanities] that ran into several volumes; there would be [no point in this.] The purpose of this brief section has been si[mply to call at-] tention to the fact that, although, as I rema[rked at the be-] ginning of this essay, the caricature of the A[merican scholar] producing laborious, enormously detailed, an[d sometimes un-] readable works of research is out of date (if i[t is a caricature of] criticism), there is still a vast amount of ind[ustrious labor in] producing literary scholarship in America [and elsewhere] which requires much more than dogged toil [and can never] justly be put in the category of what Professor [Daiches called] "useful slave labor in a good cause."

Shakespeare plays), 100 are volumes of modern European plays in translation, and 48 contain modern American plays, making a total of over 530 volumes on drama. Here the student will find Eric Bentley's three volumes of *The Classic Theatre,* a collection of medieval miracle plays, a variety of collections of Elizabethan drama, the whole corpus of Greek drama (notably the admirable series edited by David Grene and Richmond Lattimore for the University of Chicago Press), Restoration drama, and translations of plays by Corneille, Racine, Molière, Ibsen, Strindberg, Chekhov, Ionesco, among many others. Under the general heading of "literature" there are 817 texts of important literary works and 455 books of criticism and literary history. There are 271 volumes of poetry and 110 anthologies of poetry and works of criticism of poetry. There are 518 volumes of biography and autobiography, including Richard Ellmann's *Yeats: The Man and the Masks,* Gay Wilson Allen's *Walt Whitman,* and an edition of Newman's *Apologia Pro Vita Sua.* There are 239 volumes of short stories and essays, including a volume of essays and another of stories by Henry James, Thackeray's *Book of Snobs* (not easily available elsewhere), several volumes of stories by Joseph Conrad, selections from the *Tatler* and the *Spectator,* and essays by Francis Bacon, Charles Lamb, George Orwell, and Jean-Paul Sartre.

Paperbacks are not published as prestige volumes; they are published to sell. If Harbage's *As They Liked It* (discussed in the section on Shakespeare), Joseph Wood Krutch's *Comedy and Conscience After the Restoration,* Frederick J. Hoffman's *Freudianism and the Literary Mind,* Louis Bredvold's *Intellectual Milieu of John Dryden,* Perry Miller's important and valuable anthology of *American Transcendentalists,* and Lionel Trilling's *The Liberal Imagination*—to name no more—are available in paperback, it must mean that they are being bought and read by large numbers of students. Not only is a substantial proportion of the important scholarly and critical work done by American and British writers published now in paperback, we also find made available in this form, in addition to many scores of standard poets and novelists, texts of works often talked about in classroom lectures but rarely read by the student because rarely available outside a formidable volume in the library. Every student of the eighteenth century has heard about Montesquieu's *L'Esprit des lois,* but one wonders how many actually read it, or had an opportunity of reading it, before it was made available in a paperback in Thomas Nugent's translation. (And there are actually two well-edited and translated editions of Montesquieu's *Persian Letters* in paperback.) Students of nineteenth century English literature are continually urged to read Mrs. Gaskell's novels other than the popular *Cranford*—and *Mary Barton* has been made available, with an introduction, in paperback. Henry Mackenzie's *The Man of Feeling* and Disraeli's *Sybil* are other examples of works generally read about in literary textbooks rather than read that are now in print in this easily accessible form. One could mention scores of such items. All this in addition to standard works of well-known writers available often in several editions each with its own critical introduction and sometimes with other editorial apparatus also. It is an interesitng fact that teachers of English literature in British universities have frequently in recent years had to buy American paperback editions of works they needed either because they were the only editions in print or because they were the best edited.

We must remember this when we look into an American learned journal and are distressed to find a tortured article trying to demonstrate some insignificant similarity between two minor works hitherto regarded as having no connection presented as a contribution to humane scholarship, or when we see in a critical periodical an article clearly written only for the critic's fellow experts demonstrating an exhibitionist ingenuity without any real insight. If occasionally we have the feeling that American literary scholarship is an industry existing only in order to perpetuate itself, we can take comfort not only from the large number of really important and illuminating works of criticism and scholarship some of which have been discussed or mentioned in this survey, but also from the increasing availability both of standard authors and of interesting out-of-the-way works, and of works of criticism, explanation, and history, which are available *to be bought*.

I do not know how far the paperback revolution has changed the book buying habits of the American student, but I do know that in the many years I taught at American universities (1937-43 at Chicago and 1946-51 at Cornell) I was disturbed by the fact that even my best and most dedicated students bought so few books, and by the related fact that booksellers even in university towns and situated on campus were so poorly stocked and as a rule carried (in addition to best sellers and greeting cards) only textbooks ordered in advance by the instructor. The American academic habit of using as a textbook a mammoth anthology (of, say, eighteenth century English literature or Victorian poetry) that contains generous extracts of all the significant works of the period together with biographical, bibliographical, historical, and explanatory notes, has many advantages. It enables the student to possess in a single volume all or much of the important writing of the period, including many items not easily obtainable separately. But it also has an inhibiting effect. The student imagines that he has "got" the eighteenth century or the Victorian period between the covers of that one anthology, and does not go out and buy individual books for himself.

Now the buying of individual books for oneself is an important part of a liberal education, and even if the students did not sell their anthologies as soon as the course was over, as the majority of them do or did, there is something wrong in building up a library out of at most half a dozen vast anthologies. This, incidentally, is why such anthologies are almost unknown in England, where there is a prejudice against them—a prejudice that does not prevent most professors of English who visit America from England from returning with as many such volumes as they can pack into their luggage. Anthologies, it is often argued, are short cuts that prevent students from seeking out and finding individual books for themselves in order to build up their own personal libraries. There is a utopian element in this argument, but it is not altogether without foundation. The economic argument is not really relevant here, for the question is not whether the student can afford to buy many books but whether he lives and works in an atmosphere in which the individual buying of books becomes a top priority; it is thus less a question of how much is spent on books than what place in the total expenditure of the student book buying holds.

It is true that some paperbacks are themselves anthologies,

though few are as large and none is as heavy as the standard type of textbook anthology. But the large majority of paperbacks cannot be used as textbooks in the same way as the older kind of anthology can be used, and many of them are not the kind of book that could be made compulsory reading for classroom purposes. The student is liberated to browse among an enormous variety of original texts and of critical works, and this itself is of the highest educational advantage. A work casually referred to in a lecture or noted in a bibliography might be found here, reasonably priced, and the student would be dull indeed who would not be tempted at least to take it up and look through it. The paperback revolution puts the American scholar and critic in the shop window in a way that has not been done before. Even if the great majority of buyers of these books are university students rather than "general public" this is still a great gain, for students represent a higher proportion of the population in America than in most other countries—and even if only a small proportion of students are the book buyers, it still represents an advance.

There are obviously many factors lying behind the paperback revolution, many of them connected with the economics of publishing. But one factor in the proliferation of relatively cheap and easy-to-handle individual volumes is surely the modern insistence—critical and pedagogical—on the student's reading an individual text rather than memorizing generalizations about such texts from textbooks of literary history. The ousting of the survey course by the author course, the preference of close reading to generalized discussion, must have something to do with the academic encouragement of this development. So when the balance sheet of

151

the New Criticism comes to be drawn up, let this stand on the credit side: it has played its part in encouraging the publication and the buying of books.

The above discussion of the kinds of paperback now available has been most cursory; it would be a pleasant but a long and a not wholly relevant task to discuss many of the volumes at length. One kind of paperback publication does however deserve special mention, as it illustrates a growing tendency in modern American literary study. This is the "sourcebook," in which an editor takes a single work—say, Shakespeare's *Julius Caesar* or Conrad's *Heart of Darkness*—and prints it together with all possible background and source material, and sometimes also with a collection of critical essays. This dealing with a text depthwise, as it were, rather than lengthwise (i.e., rather than having it included in an anthology that contains many other works of the same period) is obviously related to the trend to close reading and is one of its most interesting consequences. On the other hand, the material made available in such volumes is not always of direct interest to the analytic critic; it is of more interest to the "genetic" critic, who is concerned with how the work came to be written and in how the author handled his raw materials. These sourcebooks often bring together in a single volume material that is both widely scattered and difficult to obtain, and here the saving of the student's time and energy is surely wholly defensible.

THE THEORY AND THE PRACTICE

One of the features of the American academic scene that the European visitor finds most striking is the strenuous defense of the humanities that seems to go on all the time. In Europe one rather takes for granted that the study of literature and history and philosophy is an important part of higher education and enriches a nation's culture. It is true that England has for well over a hundred years possessed a hard core of incorrigible bourgeois Philistinism, but this has never affected the curriculum of the universities or the activities of the "gentleman and scholar." The losing fight against the establishment of English literature at the British universities was not in any respect a fight for the humanities against a business ethic, but rather a fight for academic responsibility against what was considered mere dilettantism. But the American universities seem to be always fighting for their right to pursue nonutilitarian subjects. In the course of my years of teaching in America I was on three separate occasions a member of a committee whose object was to draw up a statement of the use and value of the study of literature. The framing of such statements in tones of the most ringing eloquence still goes on, and speeches and articles in which the phrase "the human spirit" is liable to recur can still be heard and read on American academic occasions. They are very often true and wise; often they reflect a thoughtfulness about general principles of which the European literary scholar is likely to be innocent. The American scholar is better prepared than most to defend his choice of career and champion the dignity of his profession. The English scholar would more likely than not be embarrassed if asked why he was doing what he was doing, and might reply at most with some such remark as "Because I like it."

The reasons for American defensive eloquence on the subject of the value of literary study are obviously bound up with the problems of financing universities (endowed as well as state), influencing legislators, impressing alumni, and in general making the claims of the humanities heard in a society in which science and business between them seem to be monopolizing men's loyalties. That this eloquence has considerable effect can be seen in such different areas as the activities of the great foundations and in the mass publication in paperback of serious literary texts. That the curriculums of colleges and universities are in some degree determined by the principles enunciated in these defenses of humane learning can be seen in the richness and variety of the "core" courses, the carefully designed courses in world literature and the Western heritage that are so characteristic of modern American higher education. My own experience of these courses is that they are imaginatively designed and often taught with enthusiasm and even dedication; there is an English fashion of sneering at them that is the product of ignorance and perhaps also of envy. The provision of texts for such courses has been a potent factor in that spate of publication of attractively edited texts of Western classics that has already been remarked upon.

At this point one pauses. For one cannot consider this topic long before one begins to wonder whether it has any relevance at all to the great mass of scholarly and critical work turned out in present day America. Is the young assistant shopping around for a Ph.D. subject, pleading with his professor to find him a subject that "hasn't yet been done," concerned in any way at all with the human spirit or any of the other things that the defenders of the humanities talk about? Is the latest symbolic squeeze given to *Wuthering Heights* by a critic determined to say something new about the novel at all costs (I have just read about a dozen fairly recent articles on *Wuthering Heights,* of which not more than three provide any illumination at all), are the members of a graduate seminar competitively analyzing a lyric poem until they have reduced it to a nightmare collection of paradoxes and ambiguities, is the latest checklist of third-rate articles on a second-rate poet—are these contributions to the enrichment of the human spirit and the keeping alive of our cultural heritage? Are they not rather contributions to the professional advancement of the teacher or the graduate student? However much humane enlightenment there is at the more elementary levels of literary study, how much can there honestly be said to be at the graduate level?

One must commend the care with which American graduate students are provided in graduate school with their tools of trade and are taught the necessary skills and techniques. As I have already mentioned, this is well done, much better done than at British universities, where it is scarcely done at all. But tools of trade are but tools of trade; their justification lies in what is done with them. I must confess that I have always found the dogged professionalism of the American Ph.D. students depressing. They work hard, often carrying a heavy load of freshman English teaching at the same time, but their work more often than not represents a necessary chore, a hurdle to be got over. How often, when I was at Cornell, would students come to me asking me to suggest a subject for a doctoral dissertation, and how often did I reply that unless the student had a consuming interest in a particular topic, so that several years spent in digging deeply into it would be supremely worthwhile for him, then he would equip himself far better as a university teacher of English literature by widening his literary and general experience. "Read widely, learn another foreign language, travel abroad, fall in love—do something to mature your literary understanding," I would urge. "That is much better than spending years 'researching' on a subject suggested to you by someone else." And how often did I get the same reply: "It sounds very nice in theory; but I must eat." (I am not arguing against a fairly advanced research *exercise* for all potential academic teachers of literature—to take say a year at most; but a compulsory and universal full-blown Ph.D. is not, it seems to me, the best way of producing good academic teachers of literature.)

The desperate mugging up that goes on among graduate students to prepare for their comprehensive oral examination on the particular national literature as a whole, or to scrape through the language requirement, is perhaps in some degree an inevitable part of any formal educational process, but it is a depressing thing to watch. I have examined American graduate students in both French and German (as necessary subjects for proceeding to the Ph.D. in English literature) and I know how often the student passes this hurdle with no real knowledge of the language at all. I used to be told to set the student a passage of prose in the language and leave him alone for some hours with a dictionary. If, when I returned, he had hammered out a few sentences, he was to be passed. I suspect that one could pass a test in a totally unknown language under such conditions. My experience may of course have been exceptional, but I doubt it. Only the other day we had an American university teacher staying with us and I reminded him of a period, several years ago, when he had been studying German for his Ph.D. language requirement, and quoted a German sentence to him. He replied that he couldn't understand a word, and that after passing his examination he had rapidly forgotten what little he knew. I myself regard this postponement of acquiring a sound reading knowledge of a foreign language until the graduate level as quite monstrous, particularly when the learning is done in such a hurried and superficial manner. But I am aware that the whole question of modern language teaching in America is at present in the melting pot, and that an improvement in language teaching at the lower educational levels is to be expected. I am aware, too, of the increasing number of American graduate students who receive aid from one of the foundations or from some other source to enable them to spend some time in a foreign country and learn the language properly while they are there; the number of American literary students at present in Italy, who have learned the language well, is greater today than it has ever been. (Italy has largely replaced France as the mecca of the American literary student, particularly the student interested in "creative" writing.)

It is, of course, both unrealistic and misleading to put a statement of the ideal aims of literary study beside the details of the actual work often involved. All serious study involves some drudgery. My real complaint is that far too often there seems to be no break-through for graduate students of literature at all, no sudden or gradual realization that *this* is where all their toil and training have been leading and that they are now free of the intellectual world to which they aspired. It has been observed often enough that the round of training Ph.D.'s to train Ph.D.'s to train Ph.D.'s can—and does—result in the building up merely of professional vested interests and nothing else. The study of literature in American colleges and universities is on such a vast scale that it is bound to build up professional vested interests that have nothing to do with the meaning and value of literary study as a humane pursuit. However encouraged one may be when one looks over a select list of American contributions to literary study over the last thirty years—and it is truly an impressive picture—it is hard to retain this enthusiasm when inspecting the actual habits and activities of the majority of graduate students of literature. "Do you think I could get an article out of it?" That desperate yet wistful question still haunts me. I found, when visiting Indian universities in 1960-61 to look into the problems of teaching English literature there, that the wholesale importing of the American Ph.D. system, and the necessity of getting a Ph.D. in order to rise on the academic ladder, had produced this same drive to "get an article out of it," to turn out a piece of "research"—something, anything, "you name it, I'll do it"—and the consequences there, where other acute educational problems also exist, were most disturbing.

There have occasionally been attempts made to assure a career in the academic teaching of literature to gifted teachers and humane scholars who never took a doctorate but instead kept enlarging their reading and understanding. So far as I know, none of these attempts has succeeded. The University of Chicago, at the time when I was there, promised that nondoctors could reach the top of the academic ladder as teachers in the college (as distinct from the divisions), but the whole movement out of which this possibility grew has since been reversed and there must be few indeed who succeeded without the conventional doctorate. And even if they did, they would have been tied to the one institution.

One does not, of course, want to encourage mere glibness, nor do I for one believe in the doctrine that anyone who has learned "how to read a book" is thereby automatically qualified to teach any literary work without any expert knowledge. The Ph.D. is obviously a valuable degree for many who wish to train themselves as academic teachers of literature, but in itself it guarantees very little—not even literacy. And the thought of all that plodding research going on throughout the country—the hunt for a subject, the piling up of the index cards, the ponderous writing up with obsessive footnoting and mammoth bibliographical appendixes—produces an infinite weariness.

Consider all the learned journals and critical periodicals in America, a proud company indeed; but consider too that each has to fill every issue, quarter after quarter, even sometimes month after month. There are not enough new insights available in the whole world to justify all that amount of printer's ink. But, it will be objected, every article need not present a new insight; a useful piece of hack work, a helpful job of footnoting, a minor piece of information that might some day come in useful to someone—surely these have their rightful place in print. Doubtless they do, if they are produced by someone as and when he feels like producing that sort of thing, but not if they are churned out under the pressure of the writer's need to justify himself professionally. I think, by contrast, of G. E. Bentley's work on the Jacobean stage—a vast and dedicated work that he had set his heart on doing at an early age and planned meticulously years ahead. I remember how, out of some incidental knowledge he picked up in the course of his researches, he found a pattern emerging about the respective reputations of Shakespeare and Ben Jonson in the seventeenth century, and as a result produced his two-volume study of *Shakespeare and Jonson: Their Reputations in the Seventeenth Century Compared* (1945), truly a parergon, thrown up by his other studies, yet a real work of scholarship and genuinely illuminating on an important question of seventeenth century literary taste and opinion. The best scholarly articles (only rarely, as in this case, complete books) are often thrown up as a result of wide reading in a field other than the specific one covered by the article. This at least seems a better model of the way to fill the learned journals than the rehashing of a dead thesis or the desperate working up of the results of a seminar discussion.

The literary student needs freedom to read, freedom to think, above all, freedom to lie fallow. Ideas that come to one as one reads "for pleasure" something not directly connected with one's immediate professional preparation can build up until they suggest a subject for an essay or a book or perhaps even just a short illuminating note. The direction of the research comes from the ideas, not the other way round. The foundations, in making it possible for literary scholars and critics to take a year or more off from their routine teaching tasks, are making it easier for them to lie fallow and extend their reading and thinking; but how many applicants for a grant from a foundation would be successful if they did not already have a cut-and-dried scheme of research to propose and instead simply said that they wanted a year's leisure to read and think?

So one cannot help having doubts about "the system." One comes back again and again to the fact that the training of the enormous mass of academic teachers of literature that is necessary to fill the great number of college and university teaching positions in modern America is bound to reduce the whole business to a routine. Further, more people embark on that routine than have real interests and abilities in the subject. If American literary scholars and critics are among the very best in the world today, it is also true that the "tail" is insufferably long, that there are more fundamentally incompetent people engaged in literary study in America than anywhere else in the world. There are American graduate students who achieve their Ph.D.'s who would not make the grade as undergraduates—would not, in some cases, pass the high school leaving examination—in some other countries. Again, one must distinguish between the best in the best universities and the whole range of others from reasonably good to thoroughly inadequate.

There is another point. In literary study, a man should have his formal professional qualifications behind him by his mid-twenties at the latest, so that he can proceed, while still relatively young, to cultivate the breadth of interests and engage in that wide and freely chosen reading that alone can mature taste and bring about the proper kind of literary sophistication. But the age at which a student gets his Ph.D. in

161

America today seems to be moving steadily up. Often students marry and have children before they have their doctorate, and carry on for years as graduate assistants (sometimes carrying a heavy teaching load) while, in such spare time as they have, continuing to plod along at their theses. It seems to me that the whole educational process should start earlier and (in its formal aspect) finish earlier. This of course is bound up with the problem of the high school curriculum, and doubtless I am displaying a European prejudice when I say that surely much more could and should be done in high school so that the college years could be left free for more advanced literary study. The admirable general courses in literature and thought that so many American colleges produce for their freshmen and sophomores could surely be taken at an earlier stage in the educational process; certainly it is a standing reproach to American education that freshmen English—the most elementary kind of composition courses—should have to be taught at the college level. If this were properly taught at an earlier stage, the student who wanted to equip himself professionally in literature could go ahead more rapidly and finish his Ph.D. at a reasonable age.

It is not that American literary students do not work hard and fast: they do—much harder and faster than British students. The best of them lap up everything with great speed and energy and in a few years have covered a great deal of reading and have acquired a methodological sophistication that is far beyond that of their British contemporaries. But you cannot cultivate that necessary experience in reading and responding to literature by this high-pressure method; taste is acquired by relatively slow and cumulative reading, begun early and continued without the pressure to "get it up" by a certain date. (I am not suggesting that we manage this perfectly in Britain—far from it—but our problems in Britain are somewhat different and have different historical causes.) It may well be that in the sciences it is possible for a bright student to dash through the curriculum at high speed and really master the material. In most humanities subjects this is not possible; the subjects must be lived with as well as gone through. Too many articles, both critical and scholarly, produced by the run-of-the-mill American academic teacher of literature show evidence of their authors' lack of having lived with literature. Some of them have lived with their particular subject long enough; some can write and have written on nothing else; but that is a very different kind of "living with." As my old teacher, Professor Grierson, used to say: "What do they know of Shakespeare who only Shakespeare know?"

That is one part of the picture: a relatively late start in serious reading followed by a few years of much rapid and energetic work, followed in turn by the long, long grind of the Ph.D., with little time at any point in the process for free and leisurely reading over a wide field. The result is a lack of true confidence, what I can call only a lack of being at home in literature, that can produce freakishness or the aping of the latest fashion. I have suggested that a potential academic teacher of literature should be enabled to get his professional qualifications out of the way at an early age, to give him time to read and think outside his special field before he grows too old to acquire the habit. I am tempted now to suggest that an even better solution might be postponement of the doctorate until middle or late life (assuming that a man could proceed up the academic ladder without one), so that only after many years of wide reading and thinking would a man be allowed to stand still and dig for some years in one place.

But once again, having looked at one part of the picture we must turn to another and find it very different. I have been struck by the number of contemporary Americans who combine lively original criticism, often of modern literature, with thoroughly sound scholarship in a very different field. Cleanth Brooks, for example, is both a first-rate eighteenth century scholar and a brilliant New Critic. W. K. Wimsatt is a profound scholar of Pope and Dr. Johnson and a philosopher-critic of great originality. There are many more examples. Interest in the seventeenth century and in modern poetry has gone together for some time and there are several scholars (George Williamson, for example) who have written well on both Donne and Eliot. There are many other combinations of interests to be found among modern American scholars and critics that suggest there is already a strong countercurrent flowing in this age of specialization. I have already noted the tendency of certain modern critics to believe themselves qualified to discuss any work of the past, whether they know the period or not; but this is not what I am now talking about; I am drawing attention now to a genuine diversity of interests, as when a man both edits a volume of eighteenth century letters and writes a book on modern poetry. This is still to be found only among a small minority and it is difficult to say whether it represents a real trend or, if it does, how that trend is to accommodate itself to the pressures of modern academic life.

How can one sum up? One can say, perhaps, that there

are too many people engaged in academic literary study in America for it to be possible that all the work done should be worth doing. The fools and the freaks abound, and it is not difficult to point to something absurd or fantastic or even stupid or ignorant. But one does not judge a culture by its fools and freaks—perhaps they represent the price a culture has to pay for evolving real equality of opportunity for academic study. The positive achievement of American literary scholarship and criticism remains truly magnificent.

As one thinks of the challenging subtlety of the criticism, the meticulous care and accuracy of the scholarship, of the lively and original work in the history of ideas, the quantity of first-rate editing, the definitive biographies and collections of letters, of the vast amount of work done on original manuscripts so rapidly being accumulated by American universities, of the fruitful arguments about the place of literature and its relation to recurring human problems, the investigations of myth and of metaphor, the debate about the nature and possibilities of literary history, the controversies about how literature ought to be taught—as one contemplates all this and observes in addition the increasing *availability* of modern American scholarship and criticism and of the primary texts that provide the justification for it all, one's feeling is one of admiration verging on wonder, and one forgets about the failings and deficiencies. Those failings and deficiencies are in large measure bound up with the intractable problems of higher education in a democracy. These problems have not been solved on either side of the Atlantic; different ways of approaching them, produced largely by differences in history, have given them different shapes in different countries. But whatever their shape, they remain; and

165

one of the most encouraging features of the American cultural landscape is the concern with and debate about these problems, the deep sense of responsibility for investigating, criticizing, and improving, that are everywhere in evidence.

INDEX

ABRAMS, M. H., 43-44, 46, 108
Adams, J. C., 61, 62
Adams, Robert, 32, 33, 38
Addison, Joseph, 93
Allen, Don C., 47
Allen, Gay Wilson, 147
Allt, Peter, 13
Alspach, Russell K., 14
Altick, Richard D., 86
American students at Cambridge
  (England), 119-20
Anderson, Chester G., 20
Anderson, George K., 69, 70
Appleman, Philip, 87
Aristotelianism, 94
Aristotle, 96-97, 104, 123
Arnold, Matthew, 86, 88, 89
Arthurian stories, 72, 73
Auden, W. H., 52, 127-28

BABB, Lawrence, 50
Babbitt, Irving, 80-82, 91, 97
Bacon, Francis, 147
Baker, Carlos, 85
Baker, J. E., 87
Bald, R. C., 51, 67
Baldwin, T. W., 53, 56, 59
Barber, C. L., 58
Barnet, Sylvan, 57
Barrell, Joseph, 85
Bate, Walter Jackson, 79
Battenhouse, Roy, 57
Baugh, Albert C., 69, 108, 109
Baum, Paull F., 89

Baxter, Charles, 136, 137
Beebe, Maurice, 27
Beinecke, Edwin J., 137
Bennet, Arnold, 134
Bentley, Eric, 147
Bentley, G. E., 62-63, 160
Bibliographical Society
  (London), 63
Black, Matthew W., 51
Blackmur, Richard P., 13, 18, 26,
  120, 121, 123, 124, 127
Blake, William, 84, 85
Bloom, Harold, 84
Bodkin, Maud, 126
Bohn, William E., 116
Bollingen Foundation, 41
Bonner, W. H., 1
Booth, Bradford A., 136
Boswell factory, 79, 134
Boswell, James, 43, 134, 137, 138
Bowers, Fredson, 65-67
Bredvold, Louis, 2, 147
Brinnin, John Malcolm, 20, 30
Bronowski, Jacob, 84
Brontës, the, 88
Brooke, Tucker, 50, 109
Brooks, Cleanth, 4, 7, 13, 25, 32,
  43, 44, 45, 46, 75, 79, 96, 112,
  113, 117, 118, 121, 122, 123,
  127, 130, 164
Brown, A. C. L., 72
Brown, E. K., 86
Browning, Robert, 88, 89, 143
Bryant, J. A., Jr., 61
Buckley, J. H., 87
Bullitt, J. M., 78

167

Burke, Kenneth, 13, 111, 120, 126
Burnet, John, 103-04
Burns, Robert, 83, 137
Bush, Douglas, 33, 36, 41-42, 49, 100, 109
Butler, Nicholas Murray, 39
Byron, Lord, 76

CAHOON, Herbert, 10, 19
Cameron, K. N., 85
Campbell, Lily B., 56
Campbell, Joseph, 19
Campbell, Oscar J., 56
Carlton, W. N. C., 3
Carlyle, Thomas, 102
Chambers, E. K., 62-63
Chase, Richard, 127
Chaucer, Geoffrey, 69-74, 90, 94
Chekhov, Anton, 147
Chew, Samuel C., 109
Chicago school, 94-95, 96-97, 123
Clifford, James L., 79, 137
Coleridge, Samuel Taylor, 105, 125
College English Association, 21
Colum, Mary and Padraic, 10
Conrad, Joseph, 88, 127, 147, 152
Cook, A. S., 3, 93-94
Cooper, Lane, 143
Corcoran, Sister Mary, 47
Corneille, Pierre, 147
Coykendall, Frederick, 40
Craig, Hardin, 49, 69, 74
Crane, R. S., 79, 94, 95, 96, 97
Cross, Wilbur L., 50

DANTE, 124
Darwin, Charles, 87
Dean, Leonard F., 52
Defoe, Daniel, 137

De Groot, John Henry, 59
Dekker, Thomas, 65, 66
DeLancey Ferguson, J., 136, 137
Dempster, Germaine, 71
De Quincey, Thomas, 1, 4-6, 8, 116
Dickens, Charles, 88, 127
Disraeli, Benjamin, 148
Donne, John, 43, 75-77, 99, 113, 115, 164
Doran, Madeleine, 50
Draper, J. W., 57, 58
Drew, Elizabeth, 25
Dryden, John, 116, 147
Duncan, Joseph E., 21
Durand, W. Y., 1

EATON, Horace, 1, 6
Eliot, George, 88, 135
Eliot, T. S., 8-9, 11-12, 13, 24-26, 28, 30, 46, 75-76, 80, 82, 89, 97, 101, 120, 122, 123, 164
Ellis, F. H., 3
Ellmann, Richard, 13, 18-19, 21, 147
Empson, William, 17, 45-46, 48, 97, 123
English Institute, 60
English Literary History, 58
Erdman, David V., 84
Evans, G. Blakemore, 54
Evans, Maurice, 52
Ewald, W. B., 78
Explication de texte, 112

FAIRCHILD, H. N., 144
Farnham, Willard, 57
Faulkner, William, 9, 127
Faverty, F. E., 144
Fergusson, Francis, 26, 52, 124
Fiedler, Leslie, 127

Fight between literary criticism and literary history, 100-02
Fitts, Dudley, 124
Fitzgerald, Robert, 124
Fletcher, Harris F., 32, 38, 141
Foerster, Norman, 82
Fogle, Richard H., 85
Foladare, Joseph, 4
Ford, Ford Madox, 123
Freeman, E. A., 102
French, J. Milton, 35, 40, 41
Freund, Virginia, 51
Friar, Kimon, 20, 30
Friedman, Norman, 87
Froude, James, 102
Frye, Northrop, 84, 128
Furnas, J. C., 137
Furness, Horace Howard, 54

GASKELL, Mrs. Elizabeth, 148
Gilbert, Alan, 40
Gissing, George, 134
Givens, Seon, 10, 13
Goddard, H. G., 49
Gould, G. M., 1
Grabo, Carl, 85
Grail legend, 72
Graves, Robert, 126
Gray, Thomas, 2-6, 8, 76, 93, 117
Great Books course, 70, 103, 104
Green, J. R., 102
Greenlaw, Edwin, 144
Greg, W. W., 63, 67
Grene, David, 147
Grierson, Sir Herbert, 41, 91, 163

HAIGHT, Gordon S., 135
Hall, James, 13
Haller, William, 35, 39
Hammond, Eleanor P., 90
Hanford, James H., 35, 38, 40, 43, 91, 141, 145

Harbage, Alfred, 51, 57, 147
Hardy, J. E., 32, 43, 45, 46
Hardy, Thomas, 88
Harrison, G. B., 51
Hawthorne, Nathaniel, 9, 126, 127
Hayman, David, 21
Healey, George, 137
Heilman, Robert B., 60, 61
Herbert, George, 46, 77
Herford, C. H., 62
Hildebrand, H. N., 53
Hill, Archibald A., 67
Hill, Charles J., 50
Hillhouse, J. T., 2
Hinman, C. J. K., 64-65
History of Ideas, 106-08
Hoffman, Frederick J., 147
Holzknecht, Karl J., 50
Hopkins, Gerard Manley, 76, 97, 99
Hotson, Leslie, 58, 59, 62
Huckabay, Calvin, 141
Hughes, Merritt Y., 38, 41, 42
Hulme, T. E., 76, 82, 85, 97, 123
Hume, David, 132, 138

IBSEN, Henrik, 21, 147
Ionesco, 147
Isis, 108

JAMES, Henry, 87, 88, 119, 134, 147
Jarrell, Mackie L., 21
Johnson, Alvin, 41
Johnson, E. D. H., 88
Johnson, Edgar, 132
Johnson, Samuel, 43, 79, 137, 164
Jones, W. Powell, 21
Jonson, Ben, 160
Jordan, J. E., 1

Journal of General Education, 97
Journal of the History of Ideas,
  86, 107
Joyce, James, 8-9, 10, 11, 13,
  18-24, 26, 28, 30, 127, 134,
  137
Jungian archetypes, 25
Jungian critics, 84
Jungian psychology, 126

KAIN, Richard M., 19
Keast, W. R., 60, 79
Keats, John, 76, 145
Kelleher, John, 10
Kelley, Maurice, 36, 41
Kelly, Robert, 10
Kemp Smith, Norman, 138
Kerby-Miller, Charles, 2
Kernodle, G. R., 62
Kerrigan, Anthony, 10
Ketton-Cremer, R. W., 4
Killham, John, 89
Kirby, Thomas A., 70
Kitto, G. F., 146
Kittredge, G. L., 3, 50, 70, 73, 82,
  90, 93
Knight, D. M., 2
Kökeritz, Helge, 51, 52, 60
Krouse, F. M., 47
Krutch, Joseph Wood, 37, 79,
  147

LAMAR, Virginia A., 51
Lamb, Charles, 147
Landa, Louis, 78
Lang, Cecil Y., 135
Lanman, Charles R., 80
Latin literature, 34, 123-24
Lattimore, Richmond, 124, 147
Lawrence, D. H., 8, 18, 26,
  27-28, 137
Lawrence, W. W., 71

Leavis, F. R., 32, 46, 76, 82-83,
  88, 97, 146
Levin, Harry, 19
Levin, Richard, 23
Lewis, B. R., 59
Lewis, C. S., 74
Lewis, W. S., 43, 135
Literary criticism, 92
Littauer Foundation, 41
Livingstone Lowes, John, 70, 90
Lockwood Memorial Library, 134
Loomis, L. H., 72
Loomis, R. S., 72, 73
Lounsbury, J. R., 2
Lovejoy, Arthur O., 106, 107
Lowes, John L., 91, 93, 94
Lubbock, Percy, 88
Lubbock, Robert, 59
Lumiansky, R. M., 71

MABBOTT, T. O., 40
McAdam, E. L., 79
Macaulay, Thomas Babington,
  102
McClure, Norman E., 50
McCurdy, Harold G., 60
Macdonald, Edward D., 27
Mack, Maynard, 2, 78
Mackellar, Walter, 42
Mackenzie, Henry, 148
McKeon, R. P., 94
McKerrow, R. B., 63, 65
McLean, L. M., 2
MacLeish, Archibald, 118
McLuhan, Herbert, 10
McManaway, J. G., 60
Madden, William, 87
Magalaner, Marvin, 19, 21
Mallarmé, Etienne, 21
Malone, Kemp, 69, 109
Manly, J. M., 43, 70, 90
Marchand, Leslie A., 132
Marlowe, Christopher, 58-59

Martz, Louis L., 110
Marvell, Andrew, 77
Mason, Ellsworth, 21
Matthiessen, F. O., 25
Meader, W. G., 57
Medieval studies, 69
Meen, Alan, 59
Melville, Herman, 9, 126, 127
Miller, Betty, 133
Miller, J. Hillis, 127
Miller, Perry, 147
Millett, Fred B., 30, 74
Milton, John, 9, 22, 29, 32-48, 49, 76, 141, 144
Miriam Joseph, Sister, 56
Modern Fiction Studies, 21, 24, 27
Modern Language Association, 8, 40, 54, 93, 100
Modern Language Review, 53
Modern Philology, 96, 143
Molière, 147
Montesquieu, Charles Louis de Secondat, 148
Moore, George, 142
Moore, Harry T., 8, 26, 27, 28
More, Paul Elmer, 80-82
Mossner, Ernest C., 34, 132, 138
Mozart, Wolfgang Amadeus, 21
Mudrick, Marvin, 88
Murphy, Maurice, 10

NASHE, Thomas, 63, 65
Nehls, Edward, 27
Neilson, William A., 50
New Criticism, 2, 4, 6, 7, 17, 37, 46, 60, 73, 76, 77, 83, 85, 91, 96, 97, 98, 99, 104, 111, 115, 123, 125, 152, 164
New Humanism, 43, 80-82, 85, 91
Newman, John H., 147

Nicolson, Marjorie Hope, 106, 107
Nineteenth Century Fiction, 88
Noon, William T., 20, 21
Northup, C. S., 3
Norton, C. E., 3
Nugent, Thomas, 148

O'CONNOR, William Van, 75, 76
Old and Middle English literature, 69-74, 91, 92, 93
Orwell, George, 147
Osgood, C. G., 144

PADELFORD, F. M., 144
Paperback editions, 44, 51-52, 146-52
Parker, William R., 35, 42, 47
Parkin, Rebecca, 2
Parrot, Thomas M., 2, 50
Patrick, J. Max, 47
Patrides, Constantinos A., 43
Patterson, Frank A., 38, 39
Peckham, Morse, 3
Percival, Milton O., 84
Perse, St. John, 25
Ph.D. system, 5, 7, 103, 138, 141, 155, 156-63
Phelps, W. L., 3
Philological Quarterly, 143
Philological tradition, 91, 109
PMLA, 1, 6, 8, 12, 20, 58, 87, 116, 143
Pollard, A. H., 63
Pope, Alexander, 1-2, 5-8, 43, 76, 77, 137, 164
Pope, Elizabeth M., 47, 61
Potter, George R., 43
Pottle, F. A., 43
Potts, Abbie Findlay, 58
Pound, Ezra, 89, 123
Powell Jones, W., 4

Pressure to publish, 99
Price, Martin, 78
Prince, F. T., 37
Prior, Matthew, 99
Proctor, S. K., 1, 6
Protest against literary history, 95-96, 109-10
Prouty, Charles T., 51, 52, 62
Pulos, C. E., 123

QUINTANA, Richard, 78

RABELAIS, François, 21
Racine, Jean, 147
Randall, David, 133-34, 135
Ransom, John Crowe, 26, 76, 95, 96, 100, 120, 121
Ratchford, Fanny, 88
Ray, Gordon, 132, 135
Raysor, T. M., 144
Reed, A. L., 3
Renaissance News, 41
Revolt against history, 109-10
Rexroth, Kenneth, 30-31
Richards, I. A., 97, 123
Rickert, Edith, 43, 70, 90
Rilke, R. M., 124
Robinson, F. N., 70, 90
Robinson, Henry Morton, 19
Robson, Flora, 52
Rockefeller Foundation, 41
Rollins, Hyder E., 145
Root, R. K., 2, 70, 90
Rosenberg, Isaac, 30
Rugoff, Milton A., 77
Ruskin, John, 21
Russell, Bertrand, 27

SARTRE, Jean-Paul, 147
Savage, H. L., 73
Schorer, Mark, 84, 87

Schultz, Howard, 36
Schutte, William J., 21
Schwartz, Delmore, 14-16, 26
Science and literature, 107
Scott, N. A., Jr., 57
Scottish Renaissance, 31
Shaaber, Matthew A., 51
Shakespeare, William, 2, 9, 25, 29, 39, 49-68, 100, 144, 147, 152, 160
Shakespeare Association of America, 54
Shattuck, Charles, 23
Shelley, Percy Bysshe, 76, 82-83, 84-85, 86
Shepard, Odell, 3
Sherburn, George, 2, 43, 109, 137
Sherman, Stuart P., 81
Shipley, Joseph T., 79
Simpson, Evelyn M., 43
Simpson, Percy, 62
Sirluck, Ernest, 41
Sisson, C. J., 52
Slocum, John J., 19
Smith, Grover, Jr., 25
Smith, Irwin, 62
Snyder, E. D., 3
Snyder, Franklyn B., 137
Sourcebook, 152
Southey, Robert, 39
Spencer, Theodore, 19, 49, 77
Spenser, Edmund, 58, 76, 144, 145
Spingarn, J. E., 91
Stallman, Robert W., 83
Starr, H. W., 3
Steeves, Edna, 2
Stein, Arnold, 32, 47
Steinmann, Martin, 13
Stendhal, 124
Sterne, Laurence, 21
Stevens, David H., 41, 141
Stevenson, Robert Louis, 136-37
Stoll, Elmer E., 55

Strindberg, August, 147
Stroud, Theodore A., 71
Studies in Bibliography, 53, 65, 66, 67
Summers, Joseph H., 77
Survey course, 94
Sutherland, J. H., 4
Svendsen, Kester, 36
Sweeney, J. J., 26
Swift, Jonathan, 78
Swinburne, A. C., 135

"TASTE", 118
Tate, Allen, 26, 79, 120, 121, 122
Tatlock, J. P. S., 70, 72
Tennyson, Alfred Lord, 76, 83, 88, 89, 113
Terence, 56
Textual studies, 63-67
Thackeray, William Makepeace, 132, 134, 135, 137, 147
Thomas, Dylan, 10, 30
Thomas, Edward, 119
Thompson, Stith, 144
Tillyard, E. M. W., 37
Tindall, William York, 19, 20, 30, 127
Tinker, C. B., 93
Tommasi, Anthony, 27
Traversi, D. A., 52
Trent, W. P., 39
Trilling, Lionel, 86, 120-21, 123, 124, 126, 148
Tucker Brooke, C. F., 50
Tupper, J. W., 2
Turner Forest, Louise C., 58
Tuve, Rosamond, 17, 45, 49-50, 77, 110
Twentieth Century Literature, 12

UNGER, Leonard, 13, 77
Untermeyer, Louis, 31

VAN DOREN, Mark, 49
Verlaine, Paul, 124
Victorian fiction, 88
Victorian poets, 88-89
Victorian Studies, 89, 107, 143
Virgil, 124

WAGENKNECHT, Edward, 44
Waggoner, George R., 48
Wagner, Wilhelm Richard, 21
Waingrow, Marshall, 136
Walker, Alice, 53
Waller, Edmund, 119
Wallerstein, Ruth, 110,
Walpole, Horace, 43, 135
Warren, Austin, 2, 91, 128-29
Warren, Robert Penn, 82, 96, 121, 122, 127
Webster, Margaret, 52
Wellek, René, 6, 86, 128-30
Wells, H. G., 134, 136, 137
Wells, J. E., 73
Werblowsky, R. J. Zwi, 32
Wheelwright, Philip, 126, 127
White, William, 27
Whiting, B. J., 74
Wilder, Thornton, 20
Willard, Rudolph, 73
Williams, Aubrey, 2
Williams, Oscar, 31
Williams, Philip, 53
Williamson, George, 25, 77, 164
Wilson, Edmund, 13, 30, 111, 120, 124
Wilson, F. A. C., 14
Wilson, J. Dover, 63
Wilson Knight, G., 61
Wimsatt, W. K., 2, 79, 164
Wimsatt, William K., Jr., 130
Witherspoon, Alexander, 41
Wolfe, Don M., 40, 43, 48
Wolfe, Thomas, 21

Wolff, Michael, 87
Woodhouse, A. S. P., 41
Wordsworth, William, 39, 76, 113, 117
Wright, Austin, 44
Wright, Louis B., 51

YEATS, W. B., 9, 10, 11, 12-18, 21, 30, 75, 84, 100, 120
Young, Karl, 74

ZABEL, Morton D., 26
Zen Buddhism, 81